THE
2% CLUB

THE 2% CLUB
Only 2% of the Population Have Pensions and $1M+ Saved

ISBN: 978-1-964046-83-9

Expert
Press
www.ExpertPress.net

Editing by Tamma Ford
Copyediting by Wendy Lukasiewicz
Proofreading by Heather Dubnick
Text design and composition by Emily Fritz

THE
2% CLUB

Only 2% of the Population Have
Pensions and $1M+ Saved

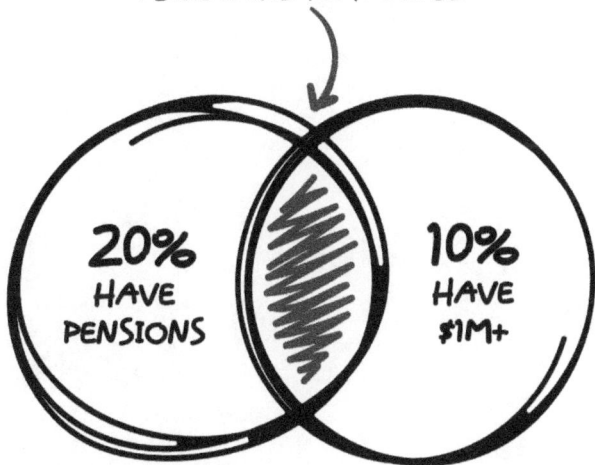

20%
HAVE
PENSIONS

10%
HAVE
$1M+

CONTENTS

Introduction to the 2% Club   1

1   **The 2% Club are Midwestern Millionaires**   5
     The True "Mr. Midwestern Millionaire"   8

2   **Having a Pension and Being in the 2% Club**   11
     How Much Is a Pension Worth?   12
     Happier with Guaranteed Income in Retirement?   13
     Lower Income in Retirement?   14
     Need for Advanced and Comprehensive Planning   15
     Financial Freedom   16
     Overview of Our 5 Pillars of Pension Planning   18

3   **Tax Planning**   21
     The Social Security Tax Torpedo   27
     What Is a Roth Conversion?   31
     The Importance of Software   36
     Charitable Planning   39
     Tax Preparation   45

4   **Investment Planning**   47
     Economic Factors in Determining Growth/
     Protect Allocation   51
     Tax Location   52
     The Importance of Professional Investment
     Management for the 2% Club   57

5   **Income Planning**   61
     Social Security Planning   62
     A Tax Storm Waiting to Happen   63
     Retiring Early with Income   66
     Tax Planning Considerations   72

6   Pension Options   75

7   Healthcare Planning   97
    Health Insurance at Early Retirement   97
    Medicare Premiums—IRMAA   99
    The Future of Medicare   101
    Long-Term Care Planning   102

8   Estate Planning   103
    Widow's Penalty   104
    Reducing Taxes to Beneficiaries   107

9   Purpose Planning—Give/Gift/Spend   109
    Give/Gift/Spend   111

Conclusion   119

A Team to Serve You in Retirement   123
    Pension Planning with Peak Retirement Planning, Inc.   125

Sneak Peek at *I Hate Taxes*   129

About the Author   147

INTRODUCTION
TO THE 2% CLUB

The 2% Club is a term I created to express how unique and special the crowd of clients we serve is.

Around 20 percent of all US workers participate in a pension plan.[1] Around 10 percent of households have retirement assets of more than $1 million.[2] Those who have a pension *and* $1 million saved? They can call themselves *members of the 2% Club.*

20 percent have pensions x 10 percent
have $1 million or more saved = 2% Club

1   "How Many American Workers Participate in Workplace Retirement Plans?" Pension Rights Center, October 23, 2023. https://pensionrights.org/resource/how-many-american-workers-participate-in-workplace-retirement-plans/. Accessed May 1, 2025.

2   John Iekel, "More Than Half of U.S. Households Have Retirement Accounts, CRS Says," American Society of Pension Professionals & Actuaries, March 4, 2025, https://www.asppa-net.org/news/2025/3/more-than-half-of-u.s.-households-have-retirement-accounts-crs-says. Accessed May 1, 2025.

This means that only 2 percent of the population will benefit from a high guaranteed income in retirement and have a high net worth. A great place to be!

Those in the 2% Club often seek expert planning to maximize their unique situation and ensure they do not miss any of the strategies that are available to preserve their wealth, reduce their taxes, and enjoy a comfortable retirement.

This book will tell you what you need to know and what you need to do. It will also describe the specific strategies used by people with pensions and $1 million or more in savings to be great stewards and maximize their hard-earned life savings.

My hope is that after you read this book, you will either contact us (or a team like ours) for assistance or gain the confidence to plan on your own. Or perhaps you'll be reassured that you're already doing everything you need to.

This book isn't meant to be an encyclopedia or to take you ten thousand hours to digest. There's no nonsense. No fluff. Just straight to the point, trusted information. It's meant to present financial concepts and choices concisely, so you have everything you need to know about maximizing your retirement.

1

THE 2% CLUB ARE
MIDWESTERN MILLIONAIRES

You wouldn't look at a crowd of people and know that among that crowd, the members of the 2% Club have done the best job preparing for their retirement. The term that may best apply to these individuals is "Midwestern Millionaire," and they're the reason I published a book about this concept.

Midwestern Millionaires are hardworking and loyal—they often work for the same employer for twenty-plus years. They are diligent savers—it isn't easy to save $1 million or more, especially when they've never made millions of dollars each year. They are frugal—the best savers, but the worst spenders. Of course, they don't have to be from the Midwest to be considered a Midwestern Millionaire. They just need to have the Midwestern values listed above, which we all respect and admire.

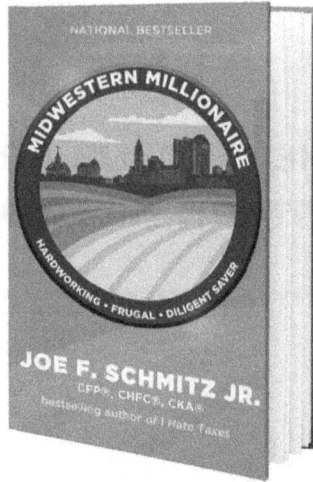

A couple we serve in Florida are every bit Midwestern Millionaires. They worked all their lives; one is a retired teacher and the other a firefighter. But since they aren't from the Midwest, they wanted to be known as "Middle-Class Millionaires." Other clients suggest we call them "Blue-Collar Millionaires." Some in the West say they are "(Mid)Western Millionaires." No matter what they call themselves, we know them when we see them. I'm sure you know and love people who fit this description. And maybe that person is you!

This is the crowd our firm at Peak Retirement Planning specializes in serving: Midwestern Millionaires with pensions, who hate taxes and want a one-stop shop to guide them in optimizing all aspects of their retirement, not just investments. Why did I decide to have our firm focus on serving only 2 percent of the population? Because we love serving people who are loyal, hardworking, and live a life of service. They're people with the same values as me, and they're like the people who raised me to be who I am today.

I grew up in a small rural community outside Columbus, Ohio, with true Midwestern values and mentality. I was taught to look people in the eye, shake their hand, and get the job done. For us, the job isn't done until it's *done*. You do whatever it takes, for as long as it takes.

We serve individuals with pensions. That includes military personnel, federal employees, firefighters, police officers, teachers, state and local employees, nurses, healthcare workers, union workers, and those who work with private or public companies that offer pensions.

Another reason I love serving these people is that the people who helped me get to where I am today were blue-collar, middle-class people with pensions. My mom, aunt, and other family members were federal employees. One uncle was a police officer, another uncle was a plumber and pipefitter, and several aunts were nurses. I have other family members who are teachers, and I have a longtime mentor who is a retired military officer. These are the people I grew up around. They have lived a life of service. And it feels good to serve those who serve us.

I didn't grow up wealthy. I grew up in a middle-class family that worked hard for everything we had. The importance of what that taught me will never be lost or forgotten.

Most people know this: We prefer to work with people we like and trust. Our team shares the same mentality as these middle-class individuals. We serve clients across the country who are attracted to our strong focus on the 2% Club and appreciate our specific pension knowledge. They tell us they can't find advisors locally with this focus and understanding. Not enough professionals specialize in pension planning for diligent savers who understand the specific type of advanced planning these individuals need. This is especially true when it comes to tax planning. Many of our clients are also faced with making irreversible and tough decisions and need to understand they have options that might be more advantageous for them. They want a team of experts who do this every single day and work with people just like them.

Many people tell us, "I don't know what I don't know."

The True "Mr. Midwestern Millionaire"

The Peak Retirement Planning team thinks they're funny. When I came up with the term "Midwestern Millionaire" to describe our clients, our team decided to get creative and produce an image of me in overalls as "Mr. Midwestern Millionaire." Fun note: Can you tell which one is the real me wearing overalls? It may be hard to tell. 😉

Mr. Midwestern Millionaire

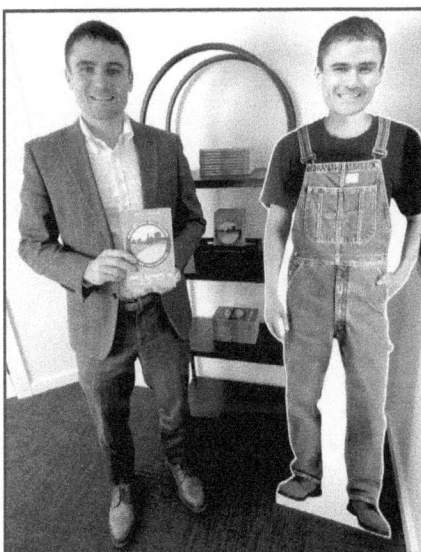

(2)

HAVING A PENSION AND BEING IN THE 2% CLUB

_____

For those in the 2% Club, take a deep breath and understand how good your situation is. You've done extremely well!

It can come as a surprise to some that they're in the 2% Club. How do we know this? After watching hours of videos from our YouTube channel (which is all about the 2% Club and has millions of views), they contact my firm, Peak Retirement Planning, and tell us. Most of them are just now realizing how much wealth they have accumulated. Their pension isn't a line item on their net worth statement. That makes people forget how valuable this asset is, so let's start by understanding how much a pension is worth.

How Much Is a Pension Worth?

If someone has a pension paying them $50,000 per year, and they live twenty more years, they will receive $1 million during that time.

As I mentioned, it doesn't show up on the net worth statement. It's like having around $1 million in additional retirement savings—and possibly more if you live longer than twenty years. In addition, some pensions have a cost-of-living adjustment that increases your pension payment each year, which could lead to even more value. Companies seldom offer pension benefits anymore because they're so costly to fund and maintain. I'm sure you've heard it from others, but you are blessed.

Happier with Guaranteed Income in Retirement?

Studies show having a guaranteed income such as a pension leads to a happier retirement.[3] We can all appreciate having one less thing to stress over when we're not worrying about where our next paycheck comes from. Since those with pensions have no idea how long they'll live, knowing they can't outlive their pension income surely makes them feel more confident and comfortable.

Keep in mind, on average, Social Security covers about 40 percent of someone's retirement income needs.[4] This helps with a portion of our retirement, but if someone has a pension, they may be able to cover 100 percent of their income needs (or even more). Social Security is the other potential source of guaranteed income for the 2% Club, but we know not everyone in the club has paid into Social Security and may not be eligible. Nowadays, with the ending of the Windfall Elimination Provision (WEP)[5] and

---

3   Ryan Ermey,"'The Data is Very Clear': One Key Element Leads to Increased Happiness in Retirement—3 Ways To Get It," CNBC, November 29, 2024, https://www.nbcchicago.com/news/business/money-report/ the-data-is-very-clear-one-key-element-leads-to-increased-happiness-in-retirement-3-ways-to-get-it/3612161/.

4   "Retirement Ready: Fact Sheet for Workers Ages 61–69," Social Security Administration, accessed May 1, 2025, https://www.ssa.gov/myaccount/ assets/materials/workers-61-69.pdf.

5   The Windfall Elimination Provision reduced Social Security benefits for those with a pension who did not pay into Social Security.

the Government Pension Offset (GPO),[6] it's more common that we see people with pensions receiving Social Security.

The other valuable thing about a pension is that you don't have to worry as much about "sequence of returns risk," where you're forced to withdraw money from the market when it's down. I refer to this as a "double loss" to your investments in retirement. My question for those in or near retirement is always this: Is there enough time to make up any money lost due to sudden, significant drops in the market?

Once a 2% Club member's paycheck goes away in retirement, knowing they have a predictable and guaranteed income stream from their pension gives them more safety when it comes to income planning.

Lower Income in Retirement?

Have you ever heard people insist,

"You'll be in a lower tax bracket in retirement?"

It can certainly be true, especially considering that 40 percent of Americans pay no income taxes.[7] But here's another fun statistic: Only 3 percent of our federal tax

---

6   The Government Pension Offset applies to those with a pension who did not pay into Social Security and received less or no Social Security as a survivor or as a spousal benefit.

7   Abigail Tierney, "Share of Households in the United States That Paid No Individual Income Tax in 2022, by Income Level," Statista, August 21, 2024, accessed May 1, 2025, https://www.statista.com/statistics/242138/percentages-of-us-households-that-pay-no-income-tax-by-income-level/.

revenue is brought in from the bottom 50 percent of the taxpayers.[8] This means the middle and upper classes are paying the bills for the United States.

The 2% Club will have a "high income" throughout their retirement with their pension income, Social Security income, and withdrawals from their investments. This combined income likely puts them in the same or higher tax bracket in retirement as when they were actively earning, not a lower one.

The Need for Advanced and Comprehensive Planning

Because of their high tax bracket, people with pensions and $1 million or more saved have taxation on their list of concerns.

> Taxes will likely be their biggest expense throughout their retirement—not their home, not their travel, but taxes.

This is why I published my book, *I Hate Taxes*, to further help the 2% Club understand the importance of tax-smart planning and how implementing specific strategies can lead to hundreds of thousands of dollars in tax savings throughout their retirement.

---

8   Erica York, "Summary of the Latest Federal Income Tax Data, 2025 Update," Tax Foundation, November 18, 2024, accessed May 14, 2025, https:// taxfoundation.org/data/all/federal/latest-federal-income-tax-data-2025/.

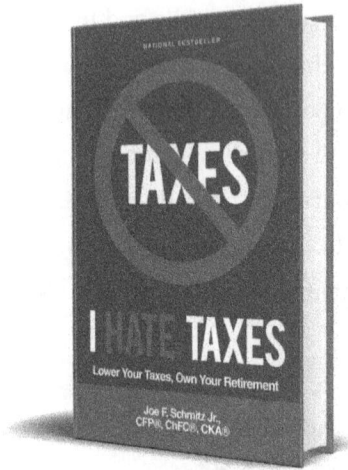

We'll discuss taxes in the next chapter, but at Peak Retirement Planning, we believe that with more wealth comes more complexity, and more opportunities to save on taxes and mitigate (or eliminate) what might have been more costly mistakes. For those in the 2% Club, we recommend a tailored plan, not a cookie-cutter approach. They don't need a simple financial plan. They're unique.

Financial Freedom

Those in the 2% Club enjoy "financial freedom," which equates to feeling happier and freer with a guaranteed income for retirement. Members of this club have dreamed of such a future their entire lives. They may have never felt it was realistic when they were living paycheck to paycheck during their working years, when most of their money went to support their family's daily expenses and to fund their pension and retirement savings.

Most of the clients we work with are diligent savers. They struggle to spend, so they're shocked to hear they can splurge in retirement or are going to have millions of dollars to leave behind if they choose. Their only focus has been on working hard and taking care of business every day. When they come to us, we encourage them to think bigger and to consider what they want to do with the wealth they have accumulated. Do they want to spend more? Give more to charities or organizations? Gift more to loved ones? Maybe all three!

The fun part about working with the 2% Club? They mostly get to do whatever they want, whenever they want, with whomever they want. With little fear of running out of money or without trouble making ends meet.

Our goal is to encourage those in the 2% Club to have peace of mind and confidence to come down the retirement mountain, as illustrated below, with a smile on their face.

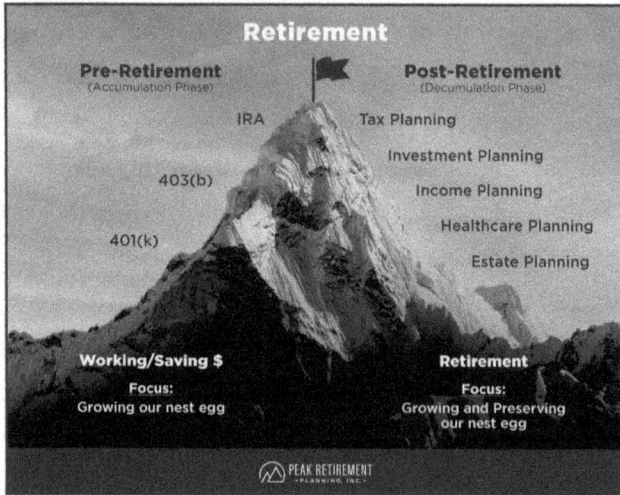

Retirement

Pre-Retirement
(Accumulation Phase)

Post-Retirement
(Decumulation Phase)

IRA

Tax Planning

Investment Planning

403(b)

Income Planning

Healthcare Planning

401(k)

Estate Planning

Working/Saving $
Focus:
Growing our nest egg

Retirement
Focus:
Growing and Preserving
our nest egg

PEAK RETIREMENT
PLANNING, INC.

Overview of Our 5 Pillars of Pension Planning

Many clients work with us because they value not having to go to multiple professionals to get the help they need to move forward in their planning efforts.

We offer a boutique, family-feel approach to retirement planning where all the professionals are in one place—a one-stop shop. We have a financial planning team with Certified Financial Planner (CFP®) professionals, we prep our clients' taxes with certified public accountants (CPAs), and we help clients get the right estate planning documents, along with health insurance, Medicare, and every other necessary expert to help our clients with any needs that arise or questions that need to be addressed. We always joke with clients that we will do everything for them except cut their grass. (Although, due to popular demand, grass cutting may become a part of our signature "5 Pillar Approach," or should I say our "6 Pillar Approach"?)

I also wrote a book on this 5 Pillar concept called *Peak Retirement: The 5 Pillars to Protect Your Wealth and Live the Retirement You Deserve.* This book breaks down the concepts in deeper detail for those who want to learn more.

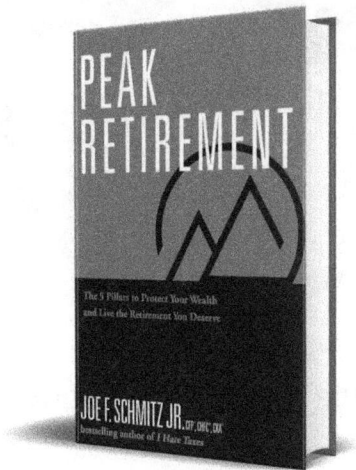

I'll present each of these five pillars in the next chapters to reveal to those in the 2% Club the type of planning they should consider implementing. As we do with every client, we'll start with the cornerstone of our planning, which is the tax planning pillar.

Tax Planning

- ✓ Use of tax software, reports, and calculators
- ✓ Roth conversions
- ✓ RMD planning
- ✓ Charitable planning
- ✓ Tax prep

Investment Planning

- ✓ Seeking protection and growth based on your objectives
- ✓ Eliminating unnecessary fees
- ✓ Professional investment manageme

5 PILLARS

TAX PLANNING

INVESTMENT PLANNING

ESTATE PLANNING

INCOME PLANNING

HEALTHCARE PLANNING

Income Planning

- ✓ Generate income from investments
- ✓ Social Security planning
- ✓ Pension planning
- ✓ Tax-efficient withdrawal strategy

Estate Planning

- ✓ Estate planning documents—trust, will, POA, etc.
- ✓ Survivor planning
- ✓ Reducing taxes to beneficiaries
- ✓ Purpose planning

Health Care Planning

- ✓ Medicare planning
- ✓ Long-term care strategies
- ✓ Planning for out-of-pocket expenses
- ✓ Planning for early retirement

(3)

TAX PLANNING

Tax planning is the first pillar of our pension planning approach and is the main focus for the 2% Club. It is essential to understand how each of the other four pillars of investment, income, healthcare, and estate planning play off the tax pillar.

Tax planning is the foundation of retirement planning for those with a high income in retirement (pension) and a high net worth (over $1 million saved).

I don't know about you, but when it comes to taxes, this is the look I get on my face:

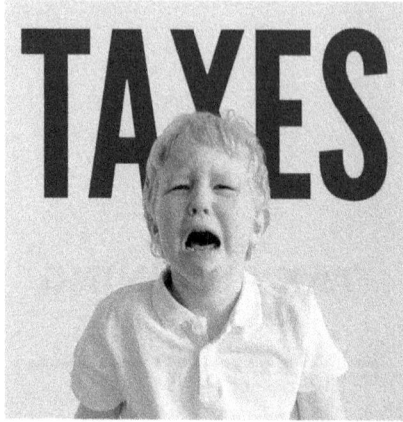

By the way, have you ever read the US Tax Code? It's extensive! The picture below is from our office lobby, showing all volumes of the six thousand–plus-page Tax Code. What's crazy is that in 1927, the Tax Code was only twenty-seven pages. It sure seems like a lot of work and a lot of taxpayer dollars to not only create but also enforce everything in those volumes.

The Tax Code provides us with plenty of tax-saving strategies and loopholes to use. But most people don't take the time to open the book, and they don't hire a team that knows the laws inside and out.

Remember, those who are a part of the 2% Club are responsible for paying a large amount of taxes for our country—simply because they have been diligent in doing the right things over their lifetime and their working years. Many of those in this category tell us they don't want to be "punished" for that. I always say that I will pay my fair share of taxes, but not a penny more—I don't want to tip Uncle Sam. Hardworking people don't want to pay their peers' taxes just because they didn't take the steps to understand how the Tax Code can benefit them.

As far as reducing that tax bill goes, the following statistic was an eye-opener for me:

> According to the Tax Foundation, the average American household will pay over $280,000 in income taxes during their lifetime that they are <u>not</u> required to pay.

When we ask our clients what they would do with that extra money in their retirement, they suddenly become creative—more travel, a greater legacy to their loved ones, maybe even a new car. What would it be for you?

As mentioned, our clients always say, "I don't know what I don't know." As retirement professionals, we are eyewitnesses to the potential costs for the 2% Club member who doesn't have a well-thought-out tax plan for retirement. Most haven't taken the necessary steps to be set up for success and pay the lowest amount of taxes possible over their retirement. If done successfully, it's not outside the realm of possibility to save hundreds of thousands of dollars throughout their retirement through tax-smart planning.

Let's continue digging further in this chapter on how to make this possible. We will cover some of the most important tax planning concepts, concerns, and strategies for the 2% Club.

Required Minimum Distributions

Required minimum distributions (RMDs) are of particular interest to the 2% Club. Most 2% Club members have saved their investments into tax-deferred retirement accounts such as Individual Retirement Accounts (IRAs), 401(k)s, 403(b)s, 457 plans, Thrift Savings Plans (TSPs), and more. An RMD is the required amount that the government forces someone to withdraw from those tax-deferred retirement accounts.

The "requirement" piece starts when a person turns seventy-three (or seventy-five for those born in 1960 or later). From that age moving forward, the government forces them to take out a specific percentage from their tax-deferred investments every year. I always joke that it's never a good thing when the government forces us to do something. The way the government receives its money is by forcing people to withdraw from those tax-deferred accounts and pay the tax on the amount withdrawn.

How RMDs Concern the 2% Club

It's true that RMDs may not be a tax concern for those who haven't saved as much as the 2% Club or who don't have pensions. For example, with only $500,000 in such accounts and no pension, the RMD may only be around $20,000. Currently, the standard deduction for a married-filing-jointly couple is over $30,000. That means if someone has gross income of $30,000 or less, they will pay no tax on that withdrawal. These thresholds are the way many people get away with not having to pay taxes in retirement.. But if their pension is going to be $30,000 or more, they're going to find themselves beyond the standard deduction and in a place where their Social Security will also become taxable, forcing them into a higher tax bracket.

The other issue with the RMD for the 2% Club is that, over the years, their RMD increases. It starts at about 4 percent of the total in the early years and can go all the way up to 9 percent or more of the total when they reach their nineties.

Also, for most people, their investments continue to grow, which means they must not only take out a higher percentage of their account balance but also take out that percentage from a larger account balance. This ultimately leads to more income at times when it can adversely affect other calculations, such as capital gains, Social Security tax, and Medicare premiums.

> Most of the 2% Club want to find ways to reduce their RMDs. They know the time to plan is now—when they are in their fifties and sixties—to avoid this "retirement tax time bomb" hitting them later.

Throughout this book, I will present ways to mitigate taxes from RMDs and even how to lower the RMD by proactive planning.

What Does an RMD Look Like for the 2% Club?

Let's walk through an example. Their pension is $40,000 a year, and they receive $40,000 from Social Security. They additionally have $1 million in tax-deferred savings, which (at 4 percent RMD) would mean the distribution could be around $40,000 in the first year. Thus, their total income is $120,000 ($40,000+$40,000+$40,000).

For someone in this situation, $120,000 may be more than they made while they were working, which is the case for a great number of the 2% Club we serve.

The problem is that taxes in retirement are different from when they're working. In retirement, they must now worry about other taxes, such as the tax on their Social Security benefit when they start receiving it. Social Security could be tax-free. It goes through a calculation called "provisional income" to see if their Social Security benefit could be subject to income tax. It can be tricky to understand, and many people miss this concept, which forces them to pay more in tax on Social Security then they need to. Let's break down how a pension plays into the taxation of Social Security.

The Social Security Tax Torpedo

What's unique about Social Security is that not everyone has to pay taxes on their Social Security benefits. Many Americans receiving Social Security don't have to pay taxes on it because their income is low enough. The higher their income, the more tax they must pay on their Social Security benefits. For those with a high pension, their Social Security may always be close to fully taxable. Some of our clients have pensions worth $100,000 or more; that alone would likely force nearly all of their Social Security benefits to be taxable. For those with moderate pensions (~$5,000 a month or less), planning for what I call the "Social Security tax torpedo" is extremely important. I'll cover how Social Security is taxed and how to avoid this potential 40 percent marginal tax rate.

The following chart does an excellent job of illustrating how Social Security can become taxed over time. The vertical axis shows the total marginal tax rate people pay from 0 to 40 percent, while the horizontal axis shows how much income they withdraw beyond their Social Security benefit, from $0 to well over $80,000 per year. If they take out just under $20,000, they pay $0 in federal taxes.

Tax Impact of the Next $1,000.00 in Ordinary Income

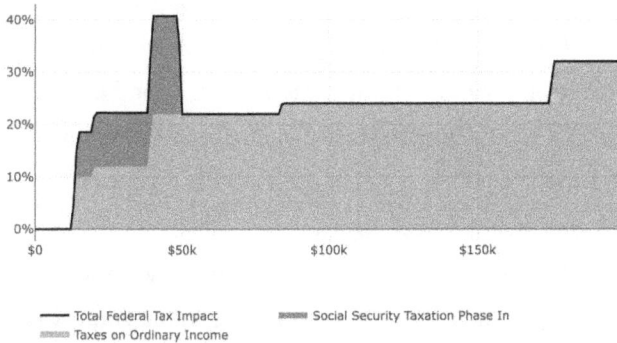

Legend:
— Total Federal Tax Impact   ▪▪▪▪ Social Security Taxation Phase In
▪▪▪▪ Taxes on Ordinary Income

Why is it $20,000 and not $30,000? As mentioned earlier, if the income were $30,000 or less, it would be tax-free. That's true until they start taking Social Security. From that time, the calculation is more advanced. As mentioned, there's something called "provisional income." It's a calculation that shows whether their Social Security is taxable and, if so, how much of it would be taxable.

In the preceding example, having a $20,000 pension would force $10,000 of the Social Security benefit to become taxable as income. But $20,000 + $10,000 is $30,000, so they would still be under the standard deduction.

Even more complex is the fact that Social Security is taxed more as income rises. It may start with only 25 percent of their benefits being taxable, then it goes up to 50 percent, and it could go all the way up to 85 percent of the Social Security benefit being taxable.

In the chart above, it is between the $60,000 and $80,000 income levels that the Social Security tax torpedo hits. This is where the marginal tax bracket could reach 40 percent or more in most cases, from a combination of someone going from the 12 percent to the 22 percent bracket and also from forcing their Social Security to become nearly fully taxable by increasing their income.

This picture can look worse if they also have capital gains, since those become taxable at certain income limits.

Let's make this a real-life example with another scenario. If someone's pension is $60,000 a year, and they decide to take $10,000 from a tax-deferred account (or the RMD rule forces them to in the future), then they could force themselves to pay a 40 percent tax on that $10,000 withdrawal. That's $4,000 they can no longer spend because it's in Uncle Sam's hands. They thought it would only cost them $1,200 since they were going to be in the 12 percent bracket, but they didn't realize it would force more of their Social Security to become taxable (unnecessarily). This causes them to get less of their Social Security and forces them into a higher tax bracket, which means they lose a total of 40 percent instead of 12 percent.

This is why diligent planning and intention—the proactive approach—are important for the 2% Club members.

For some of our clients, we try to keep them on the "left side" of the tax torpedo, if possible. The way to do this is by tax-efficient income planning in retirement, which we will cover in Chapter 5. We see many advisors and DIYers who aren't doing this calculation or are unaware of the effects when they withdraw money from their investments for income in retirement. This is one of the reasons it makes sense to work with a team focused on tax planning that has the right software and expertise to make these critical decisions for those with high income and high net worth.

What Is a Roth Conversion?

A Roth conversion happens when an individual takes money from their tax-deferred account and chooses to move it over to a tax-free account called a Roth IRA.

Let's say an individual has a traditional, tax-deferred IRA. They can move those IRA funds into a Roth IRA. When they do so, they must pay income taxes on the transferred IRA amount now.

They know they're going to withdraw from their IRA in retirement, and even if they don't want to, they'll be forced to from what we learned with RMDs. So, action will be taken one way or another when it comes to paying the taxes on this money. The question we ask the 2% Club is whether they want to pay that tax now or later.

For most of the 2% Club, Roth conversions can make a lot of sense, but that doesn't mean they should Roth-convert every dollar they have. Currently, there are no limits on Roth *conversions*—unlike Roth *contributions*, which have an annual limit. But just because we can put our hand on the hot stove, doesn't mean we should. For the 2% Club, converting small to moderate amounts over time is what we typically see, and it can be very impactful.

The other question we ask the 2% Club is whether they want to pay tax on the *seed* or the *harvest*. Coming from a rural community, I find this analogy helps me fully convey the power of the Roth conversion.

For easy numbers, let's say a 2% Club client has $100,000 in a tax-deferred account, and they want to Roth-convert today. Their total tax would be 25 percent, so they would pay $25,000 in taxes, and $75,000 would go into the Roth account. Let's say they don't Roth-convert today, but instead they let this tax-deferred account grow to $200,000 before they decide to take that money out. If we assume the same 25 percent total tax, they would now pay $50,000 in taxes. They could have paid half that if we had completed the Roth conversion today.

The first advantage of a Roth conversion? No matter what the tax rates are in the future (and most people assume they will increase), once they put the money in the Roth, it grows tax-free. Whenever they withdraw from the Roth, they will owe no further taxes on any of the money.

Other advantages? Roth IRAs have no RMDs, so the account can continue to grow tax-free if they don't need that money. They choose when to withdraw the funds and how much. This can offer an additional advantage in legacy planning for spouses and children.

Why a Roth Could be Attractive for the 2% Club

Not everyone should do a Roth conversion. If an individual approached us with $500,000 and no pension, we most likely wouldn't advise them to do a Roth conversion. As mentioned earlier, their RMD may never cause them to reach—much less exceed—the standard deduction. They will most likely take out income up to the standard deduction limit and not have to pay any taxes, so why would they do a Roth conversion and pay a tax when they could take it out later at 0 percent? They could also implement strategies like qualified charitable distributions (QCD), where proper tax planning would bring their RMD down in the future.

As we have learned, those in a $1 million (or more) category with pensions are in a unique situation. They may never find themselves in a lower tax situation in retirement, which means now is the time to do these Roth conversions. It all comes down to what they expect their income and total tax rate to be in the future.

What Will Future Tax Rates Be?

No one knows exactly what tax rates will be in the future. I always tell people that the Tax Code is written in pencil; it can be changed at any time. The rates could go lower, higher, or stay the same. Because of that, we must plan for and create what we call "tax diversification."

I'll cover tax diversification in the next chapter (which is all about the investment plan, where tax planning still has a part to play), but I'll offer a basic understanding here. For most people, we advise not having all their investments in tax-deferred vehicles but rather having some in tax-free vehicles. This helps ensure control and flexibility over where they take out money when they need it in retirement.

Many people suspect that tax rates will rise in the future, and I would have to agree. Given the current state of our economy, the growing national debt, our massive unfunded liabilities with Social Security and Medicare (especially with an aging baby boomer generation), higher tax rates seem inevitable. As a country, we continue to spend money, even on things we may not approve of or need. This spending contributes to the pressure for higher taxes. On top of that, today's tax rates are near historic lows. The following chart illustrates how the top marginal tax rate has changed since the Tax Code was introduced in 1913.

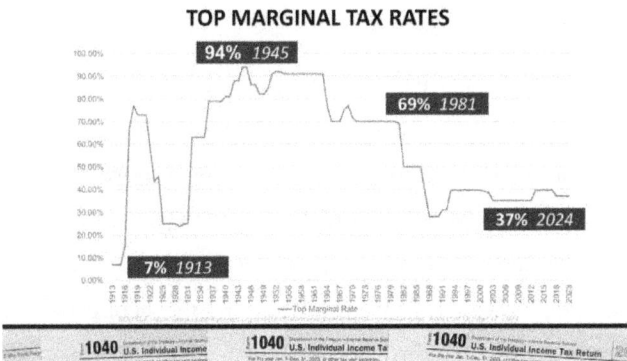

Right now, the highest rate is only 37 percent, but the highest rate ever was 94 percent in 1945. Most would expect this 37 percent tax rate to go up over time, knowing where our economy is now. Many 2% Club members see right now as a window of opportunity to take advantage of lower tax rates by implementing strategies such as the Roth conversion to pay less in taxes throughout their retirement. They believe this window could be closing, and they want to take advantage before it's too late. The solution? Proactive tax planning.

The Importance of Software

As we have already seen, and will see again throughout this book, RMDs and Roth conversions can be complex. It's hard to do such tax planning manually or to do it without the expert guidance of professionals who know how everything plays together.

That's why we always suggest working with a professional to perform this level of tax planning. You must ensure that the professional team you choose utilizes reliable tax planning software, calculators, and reports to help you make the best decisions to optimize your retirement plan. Understand that many advisors will say they do "tax planning," but make sure you know their level of expertise and how deep they will go. With planning strategies such as a Roth conversion, anyone can "guess" what the right amount to convert would be. We've had people come to us who have tried to do the conversion on their own and after realizing the complexity involved, come looking for help from a team to ensure they optimize this decision. Here's an extreme example (and something to be aware of) of someone attempting to DIY a Roth conversion. This individual tried converting $90,000 but entered the wrong amount, resulting in a $900,000 Roth conversion.

The most unfortunate aspect is that nowadays the rules have changed, and you cannot undo a Roth conversion, so they were stuck with this massive tax bill. By doing such a large conversion, they not only had phased themselves into the highest marginal tax bracket of 37 percent, but they also phased in multiple other taxes such as the NIIT, AMT, 20 percent capital gains, higher Medicare costs, and the Social Security tax torpedo. This is an extreme example, but now you understand the importance of understanding the details of a Roth Conversion.

Most of the people we see with pensions don't realize how everything plays together. They are worried about leaving money on the table or missing opportunities. They don't know that a Roth conversion can cause them to not only pay more Social Security tax but also pay higher monthly Medicare premiums, not to mention other taxes associated with having a higher income. Even for our clients, we have had to do these calculations repeatedly as things change. We look at the whole picture, so we can facilitate optimal decisions for our clients. We also want to ensure, over time, that we are optimizing the Roth conversion. It's not a one-year or one-time decision, nor is it a simple one. We must first understand from the numbers whether it makes sense to do a Roth conversion at all. Then we must decide on the optimal amount to convert along with the optimal time(s) to do it.

When making these decisions, we run projected long-term tax plans for our clients (going out twenty-plus years), and every year we refine and edit their plan based on any changes to tax rules or changes to their personal situation.

Our goal is to lower their lifetime tax bill while increasing their net worth over time. We want them to be able to spend more, give more to their favorite charities, and gift more to their loved ones.

We once had a gentleman come to us after watching our YouTube videos, reading my book *I Hate Taxes*, and trying to do the planning on his own. He said the videos and book helped him make decisions with his money, yet he still ended up paying more in taxes and penalties, and he couldn't understand why. He wanted to work with us so he wouldn't have to worry about it anymore. This man's experience is a prime example of why we always recommend people work with an expert team to help them with strategies this advanced.

Another example from a couple we serve illustrates the impact of smart tax planning. The husband is a retired engineer, and his wife was a school administrator. They came to us with a pension, over $1.2 million saved, and a simple goal: to be the best stewards of their money and not overpay Uncle Sam.

When we first met, they had no idea how much of their Social Security would be taxable, or that their

RMDs would push them into a much higher tax bracket than expected. We created a tax projection showing that, without action, their tax bill would put them in a higher tax bracket throughout retirement.

By implementing a proactive Roth conversion strategy over five years—converting modest amounts while staying in their current tax bracket—they dramatically reduced future RMDs. They now have more tax-free income, lower Medicare premiums, and less tax on their Social Security.

The husband told us, "We thought we were doing everything right, but your planning showed us what we didn't know. That saved us more than we ever imagined."

Charitable Planning

I enjoy charitable planning. One of my professional credentials is the CKA®, Certified Kingdom Advisor.

Fewer than 2 percent of CFP® professionals have this credential, so consider us in the 2% Club of advisors! It requires two crucial elements: (1) to have the expertise to pass the Certified Financial Planner (CFP®) exam (the gold standard of our industry, which only 30 percent of advisors hold)[9] and (2) to show that you practice what you preach from a biblical perspective in the Christian worldview (via pastoral references, client references, and testifying as a believer). I am proud to hold this credential and to share my beliefs and values with others.

Many of our clients who share this same worldview enjoy working with a like-minded advisor team.

This credential allows us to take a different perspective on charitable planning and help those looking to do more significant giving in a better and more purposeful way.

As for those who aren't charitably minded, we tell them they better get busy spending or giving their money to their children or loved ones, because—as the saying goes—they can't take it with them. Our hope is to ensure everyone lives their retirement the way they want.

Here's what to know: Anyone in the 2% Club planning to give $5,000 or more a year, in most cases, grab significant tax savings when they implement the right strategies. Anyone in this position who gives out of their bank account with no long-term plan is probably missing opportunities to save on taxes.

I'll explain two of the more popular strategies we see the 2% Club utilize.

---

9   The CFP Board reported surpassing one hundred thousand certificants in 2024, representing about one-third of retail financial advisors. The pass rate is 65 percent. "CFP Board Announces July 2024 CFP® Certification Exam Results," PR Newswire, August 13, 2024, accessed May 2, 2025, https://www.prnewswire.com/news-releases/cfp-board-announces-july-2024-cfp-certification-exam-results-302221137.html.

Qualified Charitable Distribution

A qualified charitable distribution (QCD) is a charitable giving strategy that people can start utilizing when they're seventy and a half years old. They can give money from their tax-deferred IRA to a charity tax-free. This can lead to enjoyable tax savings over a retirement that will allow you to either give or spend more money.

Qualified Charitable Distribution

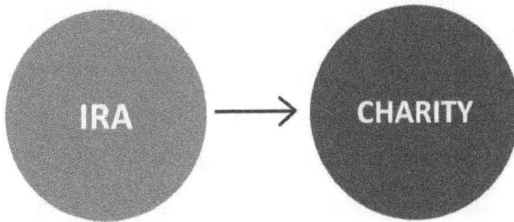

Now if they're under age seventy and a half, they should start planning for tax-efficient charitable giving strategies as part of their future tax plan, because it will determine what tax strategies they implement now (such as how much they Roth-convert and when). Most of our clients are in their fifties and sixties, therefore, we plan ahead for these strategies.

Let's say right now a client's expected RMD is $80,000, and the goal is to lower it to $40,000 to be in a lower tax situation in the future. Some people may think they have to Roth-convert enough money to get their expected future RMD down to $40,000. But if they're giving $10,000 to a charity, they only need their expected future RMD to be $50,000. Why? Because a QCD can count toward the RMD.

So if the client's RMD is $50,000 in the future (due to implementing tax strategies now like a Roth Conversion), they could take $10,000 out and donate it to a charity via QCDs, and now they're only required to take out $40,000. That means they won't have to Roth-convert as much money and can save some money on taxes (and not have to be as aggressive in the planning). This can help reduce RMDs in the future.

Oftentimes, we see people not preparing early enough (or at all) for this. We see a lot of people who are seventy and a half or older who aren't using this simple strategy that can save thousands of dollars each year. Let's say they're in that Social Security tax torpedo zone of taxable income, where their marginal tax rate is 40 percent. By giving $10,000 to a charity, they could have saved $4,000. That can add up over twenty-plus years in retirement.

Donor-Advised Funds

The donor-advised fund (DAF) tax-efficiency strategy is one of my favorites. I use it myself.

We typically recommend a DAF for those under age seventy and a half because when someone reaches that age, they can do the previously mentioned QCD to satisfy their charitable gifting in a more tax-advantaged manner. But let's say they're sixty years old and are giving $10,000 a year to a charity. In that case, they could consider gifting $100,000 to a DAF in one year to take advantage of itemized deductions that year, and then take the standard deduction each of the next nine years that they would have expected to take if they never did this strategy.

Donor-Advised Fund

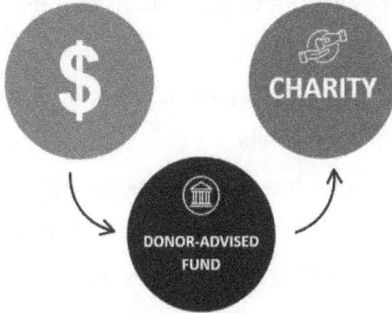

Most people nowadays don't exceed the standard deduction because it's so high. Nine out of ten people take the standard deduction, and the trend has strengthened since the Tax Cuts and Jobs Act of 2017 nearly doubled the amount.[10] This is a strategy we often use in addition to a Roth conversion to offset some of this tax write-off and start getting more tax-free growth earlier, while not paying excessive amounts of taxes to do so.

Keep in mind that you don't have to give that $100,000 to a charity all in one year. The DAF allows charitable people to give whenever they want from it. If they wanted to continue giving $10,000 a year, they could do so. The charity would receive the money from the DAF instead of from their bank account or pocket. However, they must keep in mind that a DAF is an irrevocable gift that they can't get back. If they implement this strategy, they need to make sure they are not tying up funds that may be needed in the short term.

To take this strategy to the next level, let's look at gifting appreciated assets.

Say someone has Apple stock that they bought for $10,000, which is now worth $100,000. If they cashed out, they would be paying taxes on the $90,000 gain, and it would normally be taxed at capital gains rates. By gifting this $100,000 as stock to the DAF, they have no tax to pay. This could save them nearly $15,000 in taxes, and it allows them to write off $70,000 more than if they took the standard deduction.

---

10   "What Is the Standard Deduction?" Tax Policy Center, accessed May 2, 2025, https://taxpolicycenter.org/briefing-book/what-standard-deduction.

Tax Preparation

I've always been surprised that many financial planning firms don't offer in-house tax preparation services. This is so simple for firms to do, and it improves the clients' experience (not to mention making the firm a one-stop shop). Sophisticated tax-efficiency strategies are a lot easier to plan when the financial advisor can work closely with the certified public accountant (CPA) to make decisions on the tax return. Like our firm, many CPAs have tax software that can provide detailed insight to assist in decision-making. Keep in mind that many CPAs do not do tax *planning*. They only do tax preparation, which means they would not typically advise you on strategies we have discussed up to this point.

Before we had tax preparation services in-house, we experienced many scenarios where the CPA or tax preparer wouldn't get back to us when we had questions about our client's plan. Sometimes they wouldn't even implement our tax strategies on the client's tax return, which would lead to more taxes being paid or incur penalties for which the client would be responsible.

Our clients have spent their entire lives working hard to get to where they are, so now they want to enjoy themselves and leave the heavy lifting to a professional team that can do it all for them.

Next, we will discuss our second pillar, investment planning, and explore the importance of tax planning in maximizing investments.

(4)

INVESTMENT PLANNING

Investment management becomes interesting for the 2% Club, mostly because they have the freedom to invest however they feel most comfortable. To give perspective, because the 2% Club can rely on their pension and Social Security, they may never need their investments to live on.

For the 2% Club, there are two terms we use often: paychecks and *play*checks. The pension and Social Security replace the former paychecks and provide them guaranteed income streams, while the investments are the playchecks, or money they can use for fun or to do whatever they want. Knowing this, we tell our clients that in most cases, they can take on as much or as little risk as they want. Either way will allow them to reach their goals; either way has its pros and cons.

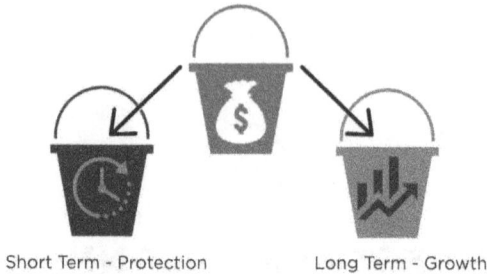

Short Term - Protection   Long Term - Growth

We think of this conversation in terms of "buckets." As we tell every client, "Every investment has its pros and cons. There is no perfect investment, or we would have all our money in it and have zero concerns."

It's important to understand that what works for one person may not work for others. It's about picking investments that align with their comfort level and plan. We never build cookie-cutter investment plans for clients; we create plans tailored to their needs and wants.

For example, when we onboard new clients, we first ask what they want to include or exclude from their portfolio. From there, we diversify the portfolio to ensure it meets the requirements needed to maximize their plan.

The "growth bucket" may consist of investing in the stock market, which could include individual stocks, index funds, or exchange-traded funds (ETFs) that all keep costs low. Some advisors or firms may recommend mutual funds, which have additional costs, so be aware that the advisors or firms might be pushing mutual funds because they get paid more for them. In most cases, since we don't get paid to offer one investment over another, we lean toward efficiency and keeping costs low for our clients.

The advantage of the growth bucket is that it could have more growth potential over time. We have definitely seen the rewards of this in previous years. The disadvantage is that this type of investment goes up and down. We have also seen this play out in recent years. Think back to 2008 when the market was down more than 50 percent.

The "protect bucket" could include vehicles that have principal protection. Many people are familiar with the different vehicles available in this bucket: bank accounts, money markets, treasuries, certain types of bonds, certain types of annuities, and certificates of deposit (CDs).

The advantage of these vehicles is that they can't lose their principal, which allows for peace of mind in times of down markets (as in 2008) and for more of a steady ride. The disadvantage is that, over time, these vehicles may not see as much growth as the growth bucket.

Now, back to telling our clients that they can take on as much or as little risk as they want.

It can sometimes make sense for the 2% Club to have more in the growth bucket. They may not need income from these investments, and they don't have to worry about sequence of returns risk, which, as mentioned in Chapter

2, is losing money from a down market. This is a major concern for people without pensions because now they're forcing a double loss—they're taking money out, which is one loss, and then forcing another loss by taking it out when the markets are down. This can significantly reduce the portfolio value over time.

It can make sense to keep the growth bucket filled if they have a high-risk tolerance, can weather the storms, and want to maximize their growth potential. Then, too, perhaps they're not worried about their living expenses, but are more concerned about leaving a legacy for their children. They keep many assets in the growth bucket in hopes of leaving more behind for them. Doing this likely won't affect their goals, and if it's what they want to do, then it could be a great idea.

So when can it make sense for the 2% Club to have money in the protect bucket? Maybe they lose sleep at night when the market fluctuates downward, and they don't want to worry about that anymore (they have lower risk tolerance). They've worked hard for their money all these years and would rather have it be more predictable and secure over time. They accept not getting the highest rate of return over time and prefer more safety.

Maybe they want to take out more income from their investments throughout retirement to either spend it, give it to charities, or gift it to children, without worrying about the sequence of returns risk. Some people in this group think about their investments as no longer needing to hit home runs since they've saved enough and have enough income. Now the goal is to hit singles and doubles to ensure they preserve what they've worked hard for.

Economic Factors in Determining Growth/ Protect Allocation

Oftentimes, our clients' choice of investing in the growth bucket versus the protect bucket doesn't just depend on their risk tolerance or income needs, but also depends on where interest rates are sitting and how attractive this option could be for them at the time.

We all know that rates fluctuate. In 2020, Treasury rates were around 1 percent, but in 2024, they were around 5 percent. Some would agree that a 5 percent rate of return in retirement with no risk is reasonable. They might then want to take advantage of that opportunity and overweight more of their investments to the protect bucket. If rates were around 1 percent, some others may think that is too low and would rather take more risk to seek a higher return.

We also see many clients taking their chips off the table, so to speak, when the market is high and repositioning their assets into the protect bucket. That could be something else for the 2% Club to consider as they plan.

Most of the 2% Club we work with sit around 70 percent in the growth bucket and 30 percent in the protect bucket. Remember, this can change based on market circumstances, as we just discussed, and on clients' needs and goals. This mix allows them to have enough to withdraw in the next five to ten years, where the principal is protected. They don't have to worry about withdrawing money from the market if they want to spend more in retirement or maybe to be prepared for any *extra* emergencies that come up beyond what their emergency can handle.

The age-old 60/40 portfolio mix in retirement might be a useful strategy for many. However, remember a pension could be considered "fixed income" and part of the 40 percent, meaning it would be acceptable to take on more risk.

Tax Location

We've been talking about the importance of tax planning, and here's another example of how taxes play a role in every other pillar.

When it comes to the investments our 2% Club members have made, there are three ways they can be taxed. Let's look at more "buckets":

The first is the "tax-deferred bucket," which means they pay taxes when they withdraw the money. This could consist of accounts such as a 401(k), 403(b), 457, TSP, deferred compensation, IRA, etc. As we know, most of those in the 2% Club have their savings here.

The second is the "tax-free bucket" (as with a Roth IRA), which means they don't pay taxes when they withdraw money from this account—it's tax free. Everyone seems to want their money here, but many people do not have as much here.

The third is the "taxable bucket," which means money is either taxed as ordinary income or as capital gains (on the profits from investments). Not everyone in the 2% Club will have investments in this category, but if they do, then tax-smart planning can be valuable.

In Chapter 5, we'll analyze how the positioning of these investments mentioned above can affect income planning. Chapter 5 is all about having a tax-efficient withdrawal plan for the 2% Club, since what they withdraw from their accounts becomes their income. But for now, I want to talk about the importance of where the 2% Club positions their specific types of investments within their plan. Are they going to be in the growth bucket and protect bucket as tax-deferred, tax-free, or taxable?

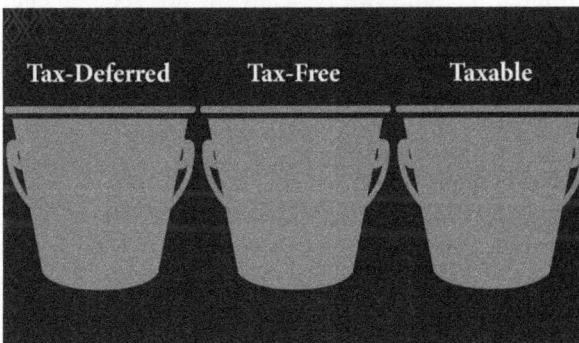

We like to place growth investments in the tax-free bucket and the taxable bucket.

Tax-Deferred Bucket

If the 2% Club wants to take less risk in their investments, we typically recommend they hold that portion of their plan (the protect bucket) in their IRA or retirement accounts, mainly because this is the highest tax rate they're likely to see. Knowing the protect bucket will likely be our slower-growing investments moving forward, we want their money in a place that is going to be taxed the most so they don't have to pay as much tax on the growth.

Also, many of the 2% Club want to withdraw as much as possible right now from their tax-deferred buckets because they're expecting tax rates to be lower right now and expecting to be in the same or higher tax bracket in the future. This can be part of their withdrawal strategy or Roth conversion plan as they seek to withdraw from their tax-deferred vehicles.

Keep in mind, we typically do not see our clients protect all of their tax-deferred investments, especially since most of the 2% Club has the majority of their investments in this bucket. Instead, as an example, if they want 20 percent protected, then that portion would go in the tax-deferred bucket, and the rest of the tax-deferred bucket would be growth-oriented.

Tax-Free Bucket

One reason we encourage clients to have money in the tax-free bucket, like a Roth IRA, is because all the growth in that account is tax-free. Because of this, we typically recommend that the tax-free bucket be mostly growth-focused to seek more tax-free growth over time.

Also, we don't expect many of our clients to withdraw from their Roth in the short term. They want to see the tax-free growth build over time and be available to take out when tax rates are potentially higher. In that case, they may have more time to buy if the market goes down and do not have to withdraw from this type of account.

The 2% Club understands the importance of this Roth IRA growing tax-free, knowing they're likely going to be in a higher income tax bracket with their pension and $1 million or more in their retirement years.

Taxable Bucket

The reasons are more complex when I say that the 2% Club should also have their taxable bucket holding growth investments, but it makes a lot of sense.

As I mentioned, the taxable investment is either taxed at the ordinary income rate or the capital gains rate. What determines the rate is the taxable investment they have put their money into. For example, if they have their taxable investment in a CD or money market, then they will pay ordinary income tax on that growth. But if they have their taxable account invested in individual stocks, index funds, or ETFs, they pay capital gains tax on that investment.

This is important because capital gains are at a lower tax bracket than ordinary income. For many people who are in the 12 percent bracket, they could be in the 0 percent capital gains bracket. People in the 22 or 24 percent federal income tax bracket could be in the 15 percent capital gains bracket, while people in the 37 percent ordinary income bracket could be in the 20 percent capital gains bracket.

I would take those favorable capital gains brackets all day long because that could mean thousands of dollars in tax savings over time.

The 2% Club could take this a step further and be even more efficient with their dollars in these taxable investments invested for growth. Once the investments have grown over time, they could move them to something like the donor-advised fund (DAF) we talked about in Chapter 3 and get the growth tax-free. Or when they pass away, the growth of this investment could be tax-free to their beneficiary—called the "stepped-up basis." This is another great example of where three of the five pillars (tax, estate, and investment) are playing together and showing us the importance of comprehensive planning.

To get even more advanced, having mutual funds as an investment creates "phantom gains," where investors may have to pay taxes on those gains throughout the year without having any choice. This can increase their tax burden when they may not want it to. That's why we recommend that people with these taxable investments invest in individual stocks, index funds, or ETFs. These investments have the low cost we've talked about, and they also allow more control over when to pay the tax or what strategy they use to save on taxes.

This concept of phantom gains may not be significant for many Americans because the capital gains tax bracket is 0 percent up to around $120,000 of income for a married couple after including the standard deduction. Most don't have this much income in retirement, so any of the gains they're seeing throughout the year are tax-free, which doesn't require any planning for them. But for the 2% Club, this is likely not a reality, and they will be forced to pay more taxes in all areas when they make their capital gains taxable.

The Importance of Professional Investment Management for the 2% Club

To summarize the above, a study by Vanguard concluded that someone can perform on average 1 to 3 percent better when they use a professional investment management team than they could by doing it themselves.[11]

---

11   Francis M. Kinniry Jr., CFA; Colleen M. Jaconetti, CPA, CFP®; Michael A. DiJoseph, CFA; David J. Walker, CFA; Maria C. Quinn, "Celebrating Vanguard Advisor's Alpha: Clients and Their Advisors Thriving Together for 25 Years," Vanguard Investment Advisory Research Center, 2025. https://advisors.vanguard.com/insights/article/celebrating-25-years-of-working-to-improve-outcomes-for-you-and-your-clients

When your financial advisor does their best work, your money could grow up to 3% more each year.

What does 3% look like over time?

$397,076
No Advisor

$898,820
With Advisor

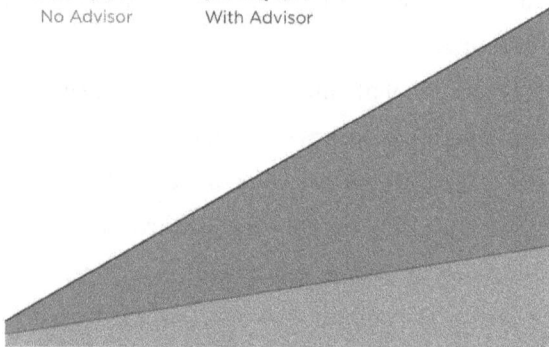

Vanguard proves this by quantifying the advantages of the actions a professional team can take, such as rebalancing at the right times, applying tax efficiency, keeping costs low, removing emotional behavior from the decision-making process, using tools and software to make investment decisions, diversifying, and following market trends. This is why we always recommend people work with a professional investment management team.

If investment planning is the only service a person is looking for, then in most cases it can be done at a low cost. But if they're paying 1 percent to only get one pillar, then they may want to pivot to a team that charges the same but does this pillar and more. We often see this from those who come to us after working with other advisors.

(5)

INCOME PLANNING

For our 2% Club, income planning in retirement involves knowing (1) how much they must and want to spend and (2) which investments they will draw money from. Although, when they have Social Security and a pension, their income issue may already seem solved. But . . . is it?

They may not run out of money, but is their income maximized and optimized? Is their income allowing them to spend more by saving on taxes and taking money out of the right places to increase their net worth over time? That is what we'll be focusing on in this chapter.

Let's start with Social Security planning for those with pensions.

Social Security Planning

We've already talked about the importance of Social Security planning from a tax perspective in Chapter 3. Now, we're going to discuss in more detail what the 2% Club needs to understand when it comes to claiming their Social Security benefit from an income planning side of things.

Now, remember: Not all those with pensions may have a Social Security benefit. You must work and pay into Social Security for at least forty quarters (or ten years) to be eligible. Unless your spouse worked and is eligible for Social Security, you could now claim half of theirs due to the elimination of the Government Pension Offset provision. We're seeing many more people with pensions needing to plan for Social Security now.

To continue the tax planning conversation we've already had, it could make sense for the 2% Club to delay taking their Social Security benefit so they have more room in their plan to do things like a Roth conversion, or to carry out other tax planning strategies that use up the lower tax brackets earlier on in retirement.

They'll also receive an increased benefit over time. If anyone waits until age seventy to start collecting their Social Security benefits, their monthly benefit will be higher than if they started taking benefits at the earliest possible age of sixty-two. In other words, if you claim benefits at age sixty-two, you receive about 70 percent of your full retirement benefit. If you wait until age seventy, you receive about 124 percent of your full benefit. This nearly doubles the Social Security income, which lasts for the rest of your life.

Obviously, that isn't the right decision for everyone, but it's something to consider. If a 2% Club member doesn't expect to have a long life expectancy, then waiting may not matter. It may make more sense to take the benefits as early as they can. That's why when people want to know the best time to start their Social Security, I say, "Tell me when you're going to pass away, and then I'll tell you the best time to take it." This is a case of not knowing if our decision was the best we could make until that time comes.

We will discuss this choice further in the estate planning section in Chapter 8 when we talk about the widow's penalty. That information may give you more insight into the best time to start your Social Security benefit.

A Tax Storm Waiting to Happen

We discussed the tax storm in Chapter 3 when we discussed the tax location (those tax-deferred, tax-free, and taxable buckets) of your investments. Take that a step further and think about not only how we invest it, but also how we're going to withdraw income from these three buckets.

Most people who come to us have all their assets in tax-deferred vehicles such as 401(k) accounts and the like. Obviously, they also have their pension, which is fully taxable since they receive it each month. As we've mentioned, their Social Security will likely be taxable as well. This is a tax storm waiting to happen. When all three of these are combined, it can lead to a very high income, as we've already discussed. That's why we want to start considering better "asset repositioning" so you can have more control and flexibility when you go to withdraw your money from your investments.

We don't know what our tax rates will be in the future, and that's why it's important to have the ability to choose what account to pull from at specific times.

There are two scenarios to consider: In the first, let's say that tax rates are high, as they were in 1945 or 1981. In years like those, I would love to have a Roth IRA that I could withdraw funds from, so that I don't have to pay those higher-rate taxes. In the second, let's look at times like we're seeing now. I would rather take income from my tax-deferred vehicles and pay lower tax on it now and save my Roth for later. I wouldn't want to use my Roth income when tax rates are low because then I miss out on the tax-free growth of it moving forward.

For most of our clients, we reposition as many of their assets to the tax-free bucket as possible without overpaying taxes. We don't want to reposition assets if it's going to lead them to pay more taxes now than they would in the future.

That's where we recommend running more advanced calculations to decide whether that will be the case or not.

If we have clients with taxable investments, we may look to fund Roth IRAs or put more toward the Roth 401(k) if they're still working. Then they can start to take money from those accounts and move into the tax-free bucket instead of the taxable bucket.

Added to that, knowing when to take income from their taxable investments based on what their cost basis is and implementing tax-loss harvesting can be important over time.

Let's go back to the example of a client's Apple stock that rose in value to $100,000 when they only paid $10,000 for it. Their cost basis is $10,000, and their profit is $90,000. Withdrawing this money could be another tax storm waiting to happen, and maybe not the best place to pull income from. Maybe it would make more sense to take the funds from another place. Or to get more advanced, maybe it makes sense to take a highly appreciated asset and move it to a charitable remainder trust, where they could seek tax savings on the gain while also enjoying an income stream for life. Even those individuals with no charitable plan in mind could find this strategy attractive. Strategically repositioning assets like this can generate significant tax savings.

It's Not Guesswork

Too often people don't understand the importance of these calculations or the strategic choices available. They go ahead and withdraw money from whichever account with no regard to the immediate or long-term tax effects, or the long-term effect on the amount of their wealth and income.

This isn't just the retirees, but also the advisors they work with, who have never done this part of planning. There seems to be no calculation or study of what makes sense to optimize their situation.

The 2% Club members have high expectations for the advisor team they trust to guide them wisely. We always tell our clients that we understand how important their life savings are to them, and we want to make sure we do everything in our power to protect and preserve every penny we can. We take their trust in us seriously, and it's our responsibility to serve them to the highest degree.

Retiring Early with Income

Since the 2% Club has pensions, they may discover that it is realistic and reasonable to retire early, knowing they have guaranteed income for life.

We have many clients who retire in their fifties or early sixties. When retiring early, we always want them to understand the important considerations when it comes to income planning, as it affects tax planning and health-care planning.

The first consideration for those retiring earlier is where they will pull that income stream from to live on. We must consider the following when planning for early retirement:

- If they retire before age sixty-two, getting their income from Social Security isn't an option.

- If their pension pays out early after they retire, then that can be helpful and cover much of the income gap.

- If their pension is delayed and can't be turned on until a later date, then the planning will become even more challenging with a larger income gap.

- If they decide to take a lump sum, then they must get busy creating their own income plan now (we will discuss the pros and cons of this in the next chapter).

They will likely need to take withdrawals from their investments to cover the income gap. This will involve specific tax planning in knowing which accounts to take from (tax-deferred vs. tax-free vs. taxable) and specific income planning to know which investments to take from (growth or protect).

The first thing to do is to determine how much they need to live on now and ongoing. What are their monthly or yearly income needs? Then they can put together a plan to ensure they have enough to make this early retirement happen.

Most of our clients have no issues with having enough money to create this income for themselves, but it's always important to go through the due diligence to ensure nothing is missed.

Now, let's find out where they could get this extra income if they retire early. It may come from their savings, their investments, their pension, or their Social Security, as mentioned. If they retire before age fifty-nine and a half, then they understand the planning needs to become more creative, as they could face penalties if they take from an account like an IRA before age fifty-nine and a half. Let's break down four ways and options to live this early retirement with ease and efficiency.

Working During Retirement

Some of you may think we're being funny for suggesting this, but how about going back to work? You may be surprised at how many retirees work in retirement. Remember, retiring doesn't mean they *can't* go back to work. Maybe they were retiring from a stressful job or one that caused harm to their health. Maybe they left a job they didn't enjoy, or they might have been forced into retirement. It never hurts to find satisfaction working and doing something they love—the activity and social side of it plus the extra income are real benefits.

Whether the work is full time or part time, they may choose to do something they're passionate about or that gives them something to stay busy with. Some may do consulting and use their expertise to make more income efficiently. Many of our clients work in retirement, because doing nothing isn't enjoyable for everyone.

Rule of 55

The 2% Club knows it: To draw income before age fifty-nine and a half from their tax-deferred 401(k) or IRA means they'll pay not only the income tax on the amount but also a 10 percent penalty. The Rule of 55, however, is an IRS provision that allows those retiring early to potentially withdraw funds from their current employer's plan without having to pay the 10 percent early withdrawal penalty—but the rule applies only if they leave their job in or after the calendar year they turn fifty-five. That said, some professions can take from their retirement account with their employer as early as age fifty (those who are public safety employees like police, firefighters, and air traffic controllers).

We often recommend that our clients move money to an IRA instead of leaving it in their retirement accounts at work, because they have more investment options in an IRA. They can invest in thousands of different options versus ten to twenty options in their employer retirement account. Also, some retirement accounts may not allow Roth conversions, whereas an IRA does, so that could allow them to get started on the tax planning at an earlier time if their funds aren't in the retirement account at work.

It wouldn't make sense to move all their 401(k) or employer retirement accounts to an IRA if someone is utilizing the Rule of 55. That's why we move only a portion of our clients' assets over to an IRA, and only move the portion over that we expect they're not going to need before age fifty-nine and a half, so that they can still get the benefits on the money they're not planning to need.

When moving money to an IRA it is important not only to keep enough money for income in the retirement account at work but also enough to pay taxes on a Roth conversion.

Let's say they planned to Roth-convert $100,000 and withhold 25 percent for taxes. If they did that from the IRA then they would pay the 10 percent penalty on the $25,000 taken out for taxes. Instead, they could manage the taxes by doing a $75,000 conversion from the IRA and withhold no taxes. And then, they will take out $25,000 from the 401(k) and withhold 100 percent to send it to the IRS to cover the tax burden without having to pay a penalty.

Too often, we see advisors who don't understand the Rule of 55. If an advisor ever tells you to move all your money before age fifty-nine and a half when the Rule of 55 exists, that's a red flag and not proper planning in most cases.

Rule of 72(t)

Another provision of the IRS regulating early withdrawals, which comes in addition to the Rule of 55, is Rule 72(t).[12] Similar to the Rule of 55, people may—under certain conditions—also withdraw amounts early from their tax-deferred retirement account without penalty. This is also known as "substantially equal periodic payments."

If you feel you need to invoke either rule to fund your early retirement, make sure you dive deeper so you understand the mechanics of the rules and get it right.

Non-Retirement Accounts

The 2% Club can naturally make withdrawals from their bank accounts or non-qualified/taxable investments without a penalty (although they may have to pay taxes on the gains, as we have discussed). Also, they may take contributions out of their Roth IRA at any time without penalty—another option to consider. In the case of these

---

12   Julia Kagan, "72(t) Rule: Definition, Calculation, and Example," Investopedia, updated August 20, 2024, accessed May 4, 2025, https://www.investopedia.com/terms/r/rule72t.asp.

withdrawals, we tell our clients to be careful about any earnings after they have withdrawn all the contributions.

Tax Planning Considerations

As I mentioned, we circle back to the tax planning aspects of creating income for yourself in retirement.

A major reason people like retiring earlier, aside from the benefits of not having to work and enjoying time freedom in retirement, is to utilize their lower tax brackets. I get heartburn when people retire early and don't utilize their lower tax brackets. They're leaving money on the table!

Let's discuss how to ensure this doesn't happen.

We've already discussed receiving income from your investments, and for many people who retire early, they take those withdrawals from their retirement accounts. As we've discussed, they can start to draw down their larger tax-deferred investments at a lower tax rate than what it could be in the future.

This, in turn, reduces their RMDs in the future, which can lead to lower Social Security taxes, Medicare premiums, capital gains, and more. Since they're retiring earlier, they're not going to have to worry about the effects of Social Security taxation or the effects of their Medicare costing more, since they're likely not at those ages yet. This provides free rein to utilize their tax brackets.

Maybe they're already getting enough income from their pension, and they don't plan to take out any more income from their investments, but they still need to consider filling up the lower tax brackets. If that's the case, then what should they do now?

Let's bring back the Roth conversion idea from earlier. The majority of our clients who retire early are looking to do Roth conversions (expecting their income to be lower now than in the future) and want to see tax-free growth for many years. And they don't have to worry as much about the other taxes mentioned, either, as they increase their income.

What about capital gains? Remember that the 0 percent capital gains bracket is generous and could allow them, while having a lower income, to sell off non-retirement investments at a gain at 0 percent tax. This is a strategy to wipe away some gain from highly appreciated investments they may have owned for a while that could be subject to the 15 percent bracket in the future.

Remember as well, utilizing the lower tax brackets and being more tax-efficient with these investments could also be reasons to delay Social Security beyond age sixty-two.

You Only Live Once

One last thought for those who have retired early, or are considering retiring early: You only live once.

I do want to share my values and opinion (take it or leave it). I don't believe retirement to leisure is what we are called to do. We are meant to have a bigger purpose for ourselves that affects others—and that purpose is lifelong. That's why I work so hard to use my God-given talents to make an impact through my work. My bigger purpose is writing books, producing educational materials for our clients, and building a team and company to serve those in need of our help.

In short, I hope I never retire in the traditional sense. I may do different things that bring me more joy as time goes on, but my goal is never to retire from a life of impacting and influencing others, whether that's volunteering, working, mentoring, or spending time with loved ones. I hope you spend your later years doing what brings you joy and fulfillment. That doesn't mean there has to be a salary or financial gain from it.

In the next chapter, I'll stay with income planning a bit. I'll address what the pension piece contributes to our clients' income plan and how that might look, especially when it comes to deciding what pension options can be taken.

(6)

PENSION OPTIONS

When it comes to retirement, the 2% Club must start by learning how to maximize the value of their pension. Most pensions come with options such as taking a lump sum or survivorship options. Most people, when choosing what to do with their pension when they get ready to retire, don't know how to do the various calculations that show them the best option to choose.

Performing specific calculations for those with pensions is what we're known for. People from across the country come to us for this specialized, tailored help when they retire. We have a client from Kansas who came to us with a state pension. They have a chart showing their potential options—specifically, the percentage of survivorship and the percentage of lump sum for them to choose. Among all the options, there were many different combinations possible. They simply said, "This is overwhelming, and I need help," knowing this was a decision that would stick with them for the entirety of their retirement, and they just did not want to make the wrong decision.

The 2% Club can't count on their employers to tell them what the best options are to maximize their pensions. Their employers *won't* tell them, and in any case, they're not equipped to do so. Many clients have told us they called HR for help. The HR department read them their options from the Employee Benefits Handbook, but couldn't provide any color or insight into what was actually the best option. Likewise, financial planning firms don't always use pension software to help calculate and maximize pension options.

It was hard to find pension software on the marketplace that fit our clients' needs, so we ended up creating our own. This tool helps us run the numbers and educate clients on the best options available for their pensions. The software helps determine whether it makes more sense for clients to take their pensions as a lump sum, partial lump sum, or ongoing monthly payments. It also allows us to calculate whether clients need the survivor benefit (so that the pension continues for a spouse if they pass away) and, if so, how much is needed.

This planning is invaluable because most decisions regarding pensions are irreversible, one-time choices. Once you've informed your pension administrators how you want to receive your pension, you're locked in. Members of the 2% Club want to maximize the pension aspect of their retirement—it's part of their life's work—and they deserve to make the best decision.

Pension Payment Options

What are those pension payment options? Our retirees' pension plans usually offer three options:

1. Monthly payments for life

2. A lump sum

3. A partial lump sum

Most people imagine retirement with a monthly amount coming to them from their pension. That's entirely possible—they can choose that first option.

But there are two other options a pension administrator frequently offers.

The second option is the lump-sum payment of the pension, and it's just that: Pensioners receive the full amount of the pension value in one payment (although it can be rolled over to an IRA to avoid taxes). They no longer qualify for monthly payments, and the employer is no longer responsible for their retired employee's pension.

They have done the job. Now it's up to the recipient to manage the reward.

The third option is the partial lump-sum payment. It pays a part of the pension value up front in a smaller one-time lump sum payment, and then the pensioner qualifies to receive the remainder as smaller monthly payments (smaller, obviously, than they would have received if they had taken the monthly payments option).

Why would we recommend or not recommend that a client take a lump sum?

Not everyone should take the lump sum, although we have seen this option become more popular in recent years. Some pensions, however, may not offer this option at all (as is the case for federal employees or military personnel). Some pensions may only allow partial lump sums and not full lump-sum options. That said, let's look at the pros and cons that could apply to most of those retirees.

Pros of Taking a Lump Sum

There are so many advantages when taking a lump sum. For one, the money is now in their pocket.

If they had opted for monthly payments for life and then passed away soon after, they may have only received one pension payment. In that case, there may be nothing left of it for their loved ones versus if they had taken the lump sum. With the lump sum, they have the money, and all that benefit would go to their loved ones.

A second advantage of the lump-sum option is having the ability to seek a higher monthly payment on your own.

If they like the idea of having a monthly guaranteed payment from their pension and want to ensure they don't lose that, they could opt for the lump sum and then find an insurance company that could provide a higher guaranteed monthly payout for life. In doing so, they might be able to outpace the pension with higher income (we often see this) while still ensuring that their spouse could continue to receive payments for their lifetime when they pass away. They could also potentially leave a legacy for their children or loved ones with the remainder (if any).

Note: When choosing this kind of insurance option, work with a financial planner, *not* an insurance salesperson. Not all insurance-only professionals have the training or knowledge to consider all five pillars of pension planning when it comes to dealing with these pension options. Also, someone who only has an insurance license isn't considered a *fiduciary,* meaning they don't have to act in the client's best interest. It took me less than two weeks to pass my insurance exam after I graduated from college—an extremely low barrier of entry for making decisions on someone else's life savings. We always educate those in the 2% Club to work with a team of Certified Financial Planner (CFP®) professionals who understand the ins and outs of insurance and how it integrates into the retirement plan.

Also note: Policies with insurance companies come in all shapes and sizes. Some are bad and some are good. A terrible idea for you could be perfect for someone else. For example, some options require you to lose everything and leave no death benefit for your loved ones when you pass away; in most cases that just doesn't make sense. Also, some options are very high in cost (think of products like variable annuities), which we wouldn't typically recommend. Again, every vehicle you can put your money into has its pros and cons. There is no perfect option. It's a matter of what works best for you and your situation.

A third advantage of a lump-sum option for the 2% Club: If they take the lump sum, they can potentially make larger withdrawals earlier in retirement or do more Roth conversions early on to achieve more tax-free growth and utilize lower tax brackets, as has been discussed. They also could have more flexibility to spend. Many members of the 2% Club like to spend money early in retirement during what is known as the "Go-Go Years." This is when they do most of their traveling, entertain more at home, or spend more nights out on the town. They understand they may not be in great health as they age and would rather enjoy these experiences earlier on. With proper planning, they know they have enough saved to do this. If they're on a predictable monthly pension benefit instead, they may not be able to strategically take advantage of the Go-Go Years.

That's why, in the early retirement Go-Go Years, they might have bigger expenses (and why longer-term income planning is key). The lump sum could give them more flexibility to not only spend more now, but also cover large expenses that may arise early in retirement. Perhaps they have high-interest debt they would like to pay off. In this case, taking the monthly pension may not be enough for them to do so quickly, whereas taking the lump sum could help them save a significant amount of money on interest over time.

Then there's the tax planning pillar aspect of the 2% Club's pension option choice. If our clients opt for ongoing payments, they'll be subject to a higher tax bracket over time and will lack control over adjusting their income in specific years from their pension.

The last advantage to mention: Taking the lump sum could also be risk-reducing. Unfortunately, there has historically been a risk (though slight) of pensions going away. Taking the lump sum isn't a decision they want to make based on gut feeling or emotion, especially if they're not sure whether the pension is well funded and well managed. For some, especially those who may live longer than the pension fund's actuarial tables predict, there may not be enough money to fund the pensions for a longer time. This is one of the main reasons pensions are disappearing from the landscape and no longer exist today for eight out of ten workers—they become too expensive to fund over a decades-long retirement.

It's important to research the pension fund to determine the reality of its solvency before making any decisions. Again, for most of the pensions we see, this isn't as much of a concern, especially knowing that we can back up issues with pensions through the Pension Benefit Guaranty Corporation.[13]

Cons of Taking a Lump Sum

For the 2% Club way of thinking, the top disadvantage of the lump-sum option is whether they would lose out on a guaranteed income stream for life. Assuming they're investing the whole lump sum themselves (with an insurance company as mentioned), then this might not be an issue, unless the monthly pension option produces more income.

Most individuals coming to us don't know how to make those calculations for themselves. They don't know how the calculations for the lump sum differ for all pensions.

Typically, when we recommend taking the lump sum, it's because we can get more income than the pension income is set to give. In scenarios where this isn't the case, we're always slower to recommend taking the lump sum.

---

13   The Pension Benefit Guaranty Corporation is a United States federally
      chartered corporation created by the Employee Retirement Income Security
      Act of 1974.

That's why it's important to do the calculations and the due diligence, and to avoid making quick, emotional decisions.

We've seen pensions where taking the lump sum meant the pensioner lost out on $1 million or more over their lifetime (if they lived until life expectancy) because of how generous the monthly payout was for the pension.

Your spouse and your health are important factors as well when considering if a pension payout is better than a lump sum. Maybe the spouse is much younger than the pensioner, or maybe the pensioner isn't in great health. In these cases, the pensioner will want to see what the survivor options look like for the pension. It may make more sense to elect 100 percent survivorship and not take the lump sum so that the spouse can have a better payout for the rest of their life. Again, this is going to depend on how the options look and are calculated.

Survivorship Options

The 2% Club must also consider the option of survivorship. Survivorship applies to pensioners who are married, where, if the spouse with the pension dies first, the surviving spouse receives a percentage (such as 50 or 100 percent) of the retiree's benefit after the retiree's death, and receives it for life.

Choosing the survivorship option is always an important conversation—but what's often more eye-opening is discussing the possibility of not selecting it. Would we ever intentionally leave a surviving spouse financially vulnerable? Of course not. Let me be clear: our goal is to ensure the non-pensioned spouse has enough income to live comfortably if their partner passes away first. That's exactly what we calculate. Through thoughtful questions and detailed planning, we help determine the income a surviving spouse would need so they can move forward without financial worry.

We take this conversation seriously. We're not trying to save money in this case, unless it makes sense. Where we can save some money is when the spouse doesn't need a 100 percent survivor option but could instead get by with a 50 percent survivor option. In some cases, this could save thousands of dollars or more each month, giving them more money to spend during their retirement years together.

We help our 2% Club think of this as an insurance policy. We ask them, "Would you get five million dollars of term insurance if only one million dollars was needed to satisfy all your needs and goals?" Most of the 2% Club does not need to overpay to be overinsured.

Our proprietary software helps us calculate what level of income the surviving spouse would need. We factor in all the other assets the client has and how much they're going to need to live on. Also keep in mind that when one spouse passes away, the surviving spouse won't need 100 percent of the income they enjoyed when both spouses were alive (usually because of fewer expenses). But still, the survivor won't get by well on 50 percent. In most cases, we find that most spouses still need 70–80 percent of the full income to maintain their standard of living on their own. Now, we do have clients where one spouse is responsible for reining in the other one from spending too much (ha!), so what happens if they pass? Well then, maybe the surviving and spending spouse will need 150 percent of what they were living on. At least, they may not need as much encouragement to spend. 😀

We also factor in the remaining investments they have and that one of the Social Security benefits is going to go away. Last, but certainly not least, be aware that the taxes can nearly double when a couple goes from filing jointly to the survivor filing single—what's considered the "widow's penalty." A couple needs to plan for this, and I'll present more details and some solutions for avoiding it in Chapter 8.

First and foremost, the pensioner can take the survivorship option so that up to 100 percent of their pension will be passed on to their spouse. But some survivorship options, like for federal employees, only allow 50 percent to be passed on to their spouse. Military personnel are only allowed to give up to a maximum of 55 percent in their survivor benefit plan.

Take the example of a federal employee, who, in order for the spouse to receive 50 percent of the pension, would have to pay 10 percent of the pension value for the privilege. If the federal employee's pension is $100,000, it would cost $10,000 a year bringing the annual pension to $90,000 ongoing. Now, if this money is needed to ensure the spouse can live comfortably and pay the bills, then we agree it could make sense.

But what if the spouse doesn't need $50,000 a year (50 percent of the unreduced original pension amount of $100,000) to meet all future needs and wants? Maybe the surviving spouse also has a pension or a sufficient Social Security benefit amount of their own. Maybe they have millions of dollars saved up that they could withdraw from and still maintain their standard of living. In that situation, I'm not sure it makes sense to take the survivorship option, and we would ask them more questions to help them decide.

Then again, what if the pensioner is ten years older than their spouse, is not in great health, and isn't expected to live as long? In that case, I would look at taking the survivor option to the highest degree, if the numbers make sense, because it would have more of a likelihood of paying out longer. That might mean they can recoup the cost to do the survivorship option.

As an example, let's say that both spouses are eighty years old, and they elected a survivorship option at age sixty that cost them $10,000 per year. That means they would have paid $200,000 (twenty years from age sixty to eighty × $10,000 = $200,000) to have the ability for the widowed (non-pension) spouse to maintain that $50,000 survivor pension ongoing. In this case, let's say the spouse with the pension passed away at age eighty. For the pension numbers to make sense (i.e., justify selecting the survivor pension all those years ago), the surviving spouse would need to live at least four more years.

Some may consider this per-year cost to be recouped in more than four years, as they're not gaining interest on this original $200,000 because they're not investing it over time (there would be a lost-opportunity cost as well). For example, if this $10,000 were invested each year for twenty years and received a 5 percent rate of return, then the breakeven now is closer to $350,000, which would take around seven years to recoup.

The numbers in my above example don't work out this way for everyone, but it gives you a good idea of what to look for in your pension.

On the flip side, if the non-pension spouse passes away first, then the $200,000 paid in was a sunk cost, and the surviving pension spouse never gets to see the benefit of it. That's a lot of money to give up (plus interest for the opportunity cost just mentioned).

When people are concerned that this may happen—where the spouse with the pension is younger or healthier—then they may want to consider getting a life insurance policy instead of opting for the survivor benefit. In this case, for the 2% Club, we run projections to see how much life insurance would be needed to fulfill the needs for that spouse if the person with the pension were to pass away tomorrow. The reason we want to project it out for tomorrow is to ensure we're thinking of the worst-case scenario. We always want to plan for the worst but expect the best.

The last thing we want is to have to look at a client after their spouse has passed and tell them that they may not have enough income to live on—that they must go back to work or work longer than planned. That's something I never want to do, and that's why we plan the way we do.

After determining the coverage needed, we would then explore whether a term or permanent life insurance policy is more suitable, considering that the term policy is less costly than the permanent policy. Sometimes it could be a combination of both types of insurance to ensure that we can get covered in the short term *and* ongoing if they live a longer time. Our software calculates all this. Keep in mind, with life insurance, you must be healthy enough to be eligible for coverage in the first place.

When someone is exploring this option, we always advise they apply for insurance before making a decision on the survivorship option. If they're not insurable or it ends up being too costly for whatever reason, we abandon this option.

Using life insurance can be a useful strategy. It ensures that a spouse will have enough money if the pensioner passes away first, but if the spouse passes away first, now the pensioner can have more flexibility and control. Maybe they keep the policies and leave them to their children or loved ones for a tax-free inheritance. They might choose to take the cash value from the permanent policies and do something else with the money. Then again, maybe they use the death benefit to cover any potential long-term care need, which could be an option with certain life insurance policies and could be tax-free.

For those diligent savers who are in the 2% Club, another less popular but doable strategy is to not take either—no survivorship option, no life insurance. That may seem extreme, as though the pensioner doesn't care about their spouse, but I can tell you that numbers and income planning don't lie. We educate the 2% Club by running the numbers for all the options available to them for comparative purposes.

Something else to note is that health insurance coverage may also be a factor in your decision-making. Keep in mind that some pensions require their recipients to take the survivorship option for their spouse to continue being covered by their health insurance if they pass away first. An example of this is for federal employees and their health insurance, called the Federal Employees Health Benefit Plan.

Pension Max Real-Life Example

Now, let's take all we have learned and see how it could play out with a real-life example. I'm going to share a case study of a family we work with and how we went about deciding what was best for them.

A disclaimer: Understand that all pensions are different, and this is by no means a recommendation of what others should do.

Age & Service Retirement Estimate

Member: JOHN DOE   Beneficiary Information:

Date of Birth	12/15/1966
Gender	Male
Termination Date	7/31/2025
Group	A

Name	Date of Birth	Gender	Relationship
Jane Doe	4/27/1967	Female	Spouse

The following table lists your estimated monthly benefit, with different **Partial Lump Sum Option Payment (PLOP)** options. This plan estimate is based on the information on file at OPERS on the date the estimate was created.

Estimated Monthly Benefit: Effective 08/01/2025 at Age 58					
Monthly Annuity Per Recipient and Plan of Payment					
Plan	PLOP Range	PLOP Amount	Member Monthly Amount	Beneficiary	Beneficiary Amount
Single Life	No PLOP	$0.00	$7,950	No Beneficiary	$0
	Minimum	$47,700.54	$7,684		
	Maximum	$286,203.24	$6,355		
Joint Life 25%	No PLOP	$0.00	$7,646	JANE DOE	$1,911
	Minimum	$45,876.00	$7,400		$1,850
	Maximum	$275,256.00	$6,171		$1,542
Joint Life 50%	No PLOP	$0.00	$7,364	JANE DOE	$3,682
	Minimum	$44,185.98	$7,136		$3,568
	Maximum	$265,115.88	$5,996		$2,998
Joint Life 100%	No PLOP	$0.00	$6,858	JANE DOE	$6,858
	Minimum	$41,153.64	$6,661		$6,661
	Maximum	$246,921.84	$5,672		$5,672

In this example, John can receive a maximum of $7,950/month. If he were to elect the survivorship option so that his wife could continue receiving this pension after his death, his benefit would drop to $6,858/month, a total decrease of $1,092/month (~$13,000/year). Essentially, John is paying a cost of ~$13,000/year for Jane to receive a $6,858/month benefit (~$82,000/year) should he pass.

One option we could look at is paying a lower cost to receive the same benefit via life insurance.

Our life insurance team ran an analysis for this couple and determined that Jane would require a lump sum of $1.25 million to live for thirty years at $82,000/year (this assumes a 5 percent growth rate of the initial death benefit over time). This required lump sum would decrease each year. In other words, after ten years, Jane would only need $1 million to live on moving forward. After twenty years, she would only require $600,000.This was best accomplished by stacking permanent and term life insurance policies. Since Jane requires $600,000 for the final ten years, we would want a policy with a value close to this amount. For years one through ten, we would want to purchase term insurance with a $650,000 death benefit, and for years ten through twenty, we would need an additional $400,000 over and above the $600,000 permanent policy. This results in three policies being purchased, making sure that Jane is the beneficiary for a total of $1.25 million in years one through ten, $1 million in years eleven through twenty, and $600,000 in years twenty-one through thirty.

Ten-year term: $250,000
Twenty-year term: $400,000
Permanent: $600,000

In this example, we could fund all these policies for under $1,000/month (as opposed to the $1,100/month baked into the pension plan).

After purchasing life insurance, John and Jane can select the higher income option ($7,950/month) and then purchase life insurance for $1,000/month, bringing their net income to $6,950/month. Should John pass, Jane will have more than the $6,858/month that would have been provided if they had elected the survivor option. This provides the coverage needed, with a higher income until John passes, and better options for them, as we talked about earlier.

In addition to providing a better survivorship option, we can maximize the partial lump sum amount. John can take a partial lump sum of up to $286,000 at the cost of $1,595/month in income or ~$19,000/year. John and Jane don't need the extra income and want to use these funds for legacy goals, so in that case, they must ask themselves if they should take the $19,000 a year to invest or take the $286,000 up front to invest.

At his age, John's life expectancy is eighty-three, or twenty-five more years. If we took the $19,000 a year at a 7 percent rate of return (ROR), that would result in $1.2 million at the end of twenty-five years. What ROR would we need to turn the $286,000 into $1.2 million? Only a 5.9 percent ROR over twenty-five years. In this case, John and Jane decided to take the lump sum to invest. They also liked the idea that if they pass away earlier than twenty-five years, then the numbers would look even better for them if they take the lump sum since that money is now in their pockets.

In the end, John and Jane will take the $286,000 partial lump-sum option with no survivor option. We will put the $286,000 into an accumulation vehicle within an IRA so it isn't a huge taxable event. This will allow them to make withdrawals from it, and we will use part of the $6,355/month benefit to pay for life insurance to make sure that Jane will have at least $5,672/month in the event of John's passing (assuming he passed away today).

For those with pensions, this is the type of calculation that gives them the power to understand their options and see them as real numbers.

Pension Calculations and Interest Rates

Oftentimes, calculating the lump-sum option on the pension is based on the expected interest rates. We have a fun example to show why this is important to consider when planning.

We had a client who could take an extra $100,000 in his lump sum if he retired tomorrow, but if he waited until next year to retire, his lump sum pension would miss out on that $100,000. And knowing that he made $100,000 a year, he would basically have worked the next year for no benefit since he would have lost the extra opportunity in his lump sum pension. In the end, he decided to retire that day and take advantage of the higher-sum option and not have to worry about working "for free," (so to speak) the entire next year. Keep in mind that when interest rates go up, lump sum amounts go down. And when interest rates go down, lump sum amounts go up. This can be important when deciding when you retire. Note that interest rates do not change the monthly payment options you have as those are fixed and typically decided upon based on years of service and the salary you earned.

Run Your Numbers

When considering income scenarios, we always recommend running multiple calculations to ensure the best decision. This is obviously not a decision to guess at. Ensure there is thorough due diligence and run complete numbers to evaluate what could be best will lead to more success over time.

We also have people come to us who either say they're going to take the lump sum no matter what, or they're going to take the monthly pension no matter what. That's foolish without information and without exploring all options. They could be missing out on having a lot of extra money in their pocket over time, not only for them but for their loved ones.

There are pros and cons to every decision, and some decisions will make more sense for some people's circumstances and goals than others. We encourage those with pensions to perform their due diligence, run their numbers, and work with a team of professionals who know how this all works together to ensure that they make the right decisions.

(7)

HEALTHCARE PLANNING

Healthcare planning is a nonnegotiable need in our country nowadays for those in retirement, for two reasons: (1) medical services in this country are among the world's most expensive, and (2) aging people require more healthcare services than they did in their younger years.

Health Insurance at Early Retirement

For those 2% Club members interested in and able to retire early (i.e., before age sixty-five when Medicare starts for everyone), their last employer may not insure them after they retire or resign, leaving them with a gap in their health insurance coverage that needs to be filled.

When they retire early, the 2% Club needs to plan not only how they'll get the income they need but also how they'll insure their health needs.

If their employer offers them health insurance after retirement to span the gap until Medicare, they can consider themselves blessed and should be excited. This will save them lots of money and will likely be good coverage (as in most cases we experience).

For those who don't have continuous health insurance coverage, they can consider having one spouse continue to work, which provides both of them with health insurance. We've even seen clients continue working enough part-time hours or decide to continue full time with an employer for the health insurance coverage.

For those who want to retire and whose employers don't offer insurance, shopping the marketplace is their best option. For our clients, we have a health insurance specialist on our team to ensure they get the right coverage for the right price before Medicare kicks in. Then, when Medicare kicks in, we help them shop for the right supplemental Medicare plan in addition to Medicare Parts A and B.

The health insurance issue is a pivotal piece of the 5 Pillars of pension planning. It means our 2% Club must be strategic with the tax planning and income planning they do. There are many moving parts, and it will be different for everyone, depending on their specific situation.

Medicare Premiums—IRMAA

Medicare premiums have increased significantly since the program's inception in 1966.[14]

Most people are unaware of the gradual increase in premiums the program has made over time. They are also unaware that their Medicare premiums are based on their income of the prior two years before age sixty-five and become eligible for Medicare. Someone who stopped earning at age sixty-two will pay less in Medicare premiums than their neighbor who earned the same annual salary but earned it right up to age sixty-five.

IRMAA is the Income-Related Monthly Adjustment Amount, where the "amount" is your monthly Medicare premium amount. Therefore, as high earners, the 2% Club is worried about how to avoid paying that higher amount in Medicare premiums.

I don't blame them. It isn't necessarily fair since everyone gets the same Medicare coverage when they turn sixty-five, whatever premium amount they pay. That means when the 2% Club earns well and up to age sixty-five, they get the same coverage but often must pay double, triple, or more than what their peers are paying.

I don't think it's fair for those who have been diligent savers and have made the right decisions over their lifetime

---

14   Rachel Nania, "Medicare Part B Premium to Increase in 2025," AARP, November 11, 2024, accessed May 6, 2025, https://www.aarp.org/medicare/medicare-part-b-premium-increase-2025/.

to be responsible for paying more of the healthcare costs for everyone. Savers are being penalized, and those who haven't saved are being rewarded.

To bring a more positive light to this conversation, there are strategies the 2% Club can use to lessen their Medicare premiums over time. The earlier they can start planning, the better.

If our 2% Club member is under age sixty-three, they need to understand that they don't have to worry about these increased costs for Medicare premiums when they do Roth conversions and other tax planning strategies. This could allow them more room to be more aggressive in their approach without having to pay more in Medicare premiums.

Now, for some of our clients who are sixty-three or older, it could still be useful to pay more in Medicare premiums over maybe a few years to allow them to pay less in Medicare premiums over their lifetime. So you want to ensure you do the calculation to see what makes sense.

Note: It's possible to file an appeal to Medicare (by filing form SSA-44) and not have to pay the higher cost for Medicare for that year if someone has had a life-changing event, such as retirement. Medicare has a list of qualifying events, and we've had great success getting this approved for our clients and saving them Medicare costs.

The Future of Medicare

We've heard some uncertainty in the media about Medicare and Social Security. Because of this we like to educate people on the future outlook of Medicare.

Like Social Security, Medicare is in trouble. It is underfunded and under great stress from those turning sixty-five and older, with a higher need for healthcare. Ten thousand people turn sixty-five every day;[15] that has happened for the last ten years and will continue for the next ten years. Baby boomers are getting to the age of needing more healthcare, and so I must ask: "Where do we get the money to pay for this?"

Healthcare costs are increasing significantly, and there's nothing we can do about it. Those in the 2% Club should always prepare based on the assumption that costs could continue to go up. This means they're going to try to keep their income lower, because that's how Medicare premiums are calculated. Not only will Medicare potentially continue increasing the cost, but it could also decrease the income tiers that determine how much we must pay.

Being in the 2% Club means being targeted more than most when it comes to this Medicare premium. Knowing your income from your guaranteed sources will

---

15   Brian J. O'Connor, "Over 12,000 Americans Will Turn 65 Every Day in 2024. Are You Ready For Retirement?" SmartAsset, Yahoo! Finance, April 19, 2024, https://finance.yahoo.com/news/over-12-000-americans-turn-133334982.html.

always be higher and having a higher investment total only makes it worse.

Long-Term Care Planning

Medicare isn't long-term healthcare. It will cover most needs, such as doctor consultations, lab work, and preventive exams. Its coverage includes hospitalization needs, but only for up to thirty days. On day thirty-one, you enter into what is called "long-term care," at your cost. There is a greater than 70 percent chance that someone who is sixty-five or older will need long-term care.[16]

Many people think of long-term care insurance when they think of long-term care planning. For many of the 2% Club we serve, we haven't seen long-term care insurance to be as advantageous recently. This is because the 2% Club can often self-insure—they have a high enough income from their pension and Social Security, and they have extra investments to cover emergencies like this.

The decisive planning comes from ensuring we are protecting and structuring their investments strategically in case they need to take large withdrawals for things like healthcare. We pay attention to market protection, but also to being tax-efficient with those larger withdrawals that can force them to pay more in taxes.

---

16   Genworth's cost of care survey chart for your personal calculations. "Calculate the Cost of Long-Term Care Near You," CareScout, accessed May 6, 2025, https://stg-origin.genworth.com/aging-and-you/finances/cost-of-care.html.

8

ESTATE PLANNING

Estate planning is our fifth pillar of focus for which the 2% Club must prepare and have a plan.

When people think of estate planning, they might think of documents such as a last will and testament, a power of attorney for healthcare decisions and financial affairs, and perhaps a trust. These are all vitally important to consider and have in place, not just for our clients' well-being and purpose but also for their family members' peace of mind.

Now, the documents are straightforward and easy to put in place. This is something we help our clients facilitate in-house to ensure they get that one-stop shop service. We always recommend that your financial planning firm be involved with this to ensure true collaboration. For the 2% Club, they must also think beyond just having estate planning documents in place. They need intentional estate planning help with taxes when transferring assets to loved ones upon passing. It's one of the most worrisome concerns we see from the 2% Club. They don't want to have worked for their abundance their entire lives, only to see Uncle Sam receive more of it than their designated beneficiaries.

Widow's Penalty

Many of our married 2% Club members fear the widow's penalty that I mentioned in Chapter 6. The widow's penalty is about taxes, especially in the year of the spouse's death, and it can be a severe tax blow. It can be costly for clients in the 2% Club since it also means the surviving spouse will be left paying more in taxes and have less income over their retirement.

Let's see why this widow's penalty is so severe. There are four main considerations for the 2% Club:

1. More taxes to pay.

A 2% Club member may have to pay nearly double the amount of taxes when the first spouse passes away. This is because, effective in the year after death, the tax brackets go from married filing jointly to single. This could also force them to pay more on their Social Security tax. It may also force them to pay more on their Medicare premiums since the income tiers used to calculate those are lower.

2. Less income being received.

When one spouse passes away, the lower of the two Social Security benefits goes away. This will cause a permanent loss of income that the widowed spouse will have to find a way to replace.

3. Potential loss of a pension.

We've already broken down the pension survivorship options, so now you know what to look for when making that decision.

4. What to do next.

Have a team working for you. We often work with families where one spouse is more involved in the financial decision-making process than the other. Having a team in place can ensure the surviving spouse isn't overwhelmed or taken advantage of without the guidance of the main financial decision-maker.

We help surviving spouses via proactive planning, with several considerations: First, it's about income. We need to ensure that the spouse will have enough throughout retirement—whether that's by ensuring that the pension survivorship option was selected, having enough life insurance coverage in place, or having enough from investments to self-insure.

Second, it's about robust tax planning. We employ strategies like a Roth conversion, where they can pay the taxes when they're married and both alive. The surviving spouse can take money from the Roth IRA tax-free and avoid the higher tax brackets associated with being single.

Third, it's about Social Security. We talked about the pros and cons of taking Social Security at different ages, but a reason to take Social Security at age seventy might be to receive the highest survivor benefit (since the surviving spouse will get the higher of the two benefits).

Finally, it's about the surviving spouse. A proactive planning concern that comes from losing a spouse is ensuring that the surviving spouse has a trusted team to help them move forward. We work with a lot of "DIY planners," where one of the spouses has done a lot of planning on their own over the years, or taken more of a proactive and intentional approach to understanding their money matters. There's only one problem: The management and DIY organizing of their finances may not have been fully shared with the spouse.

This is why we encourage both spouses to sit with us in all our meetings, from the beginning. They both need to know who to go to in an emergency, as well as for future needs. Our 2% Club members don't leave their spouses in a vulnerable position of not knowing who their trusted team is. This is one of the most important reasons people work with us.

Reducing Taxes to Beneficiaries

Many in the 2% Club know that they have enough wealth to not only provide for their lifetime but also provide for their spouse. They now want to think even further ahead about leaving money to their loved ones, which could include their children. When they want to leave money to their loved ones, the time to start planning is now, especially when it comes to their retirement accounts, such as the IRA or employer retirement plans.

Withdrawal Rules

The rules around these retirement plans have changed in recent times, which makes it less advantageous for the 2% Club to leave their retirement accounts to their children or grandchildren. The old rules stated that heirs could take withdrawals from those retirement accounts over their lifetime. That meant they could take smaller withdrawals and calculate their income tax burden accordingly. Not so anymore. It must be withdrawn within ten years now.

Of concern for the 2% Club is their large amount of tax-deferred dollars, which will force their beneficiaries to take out large withdrawals in a shorter number of years than under the old rules. If the beneficiaries are high income earners when they receive their bequest, they face a potentially higher tax bracket. And if tax rates rise in the future, their tax picture could worsen.

One of the best ways to plan for this is by doing Roth conversions now. Take note, however, that Roth conversions may not always make sense in this legacy scenario, especially if you're going to have a higher income in retirement and your kids might not.

Perhaps the heirs won't have a pension or won't be making much money at the time of the withdrawals. In that case, it may make more sense to leave the accounts to the kids in tax-deferred status so they can pay it at their lower income tax rate. Don't forget, though, there is no RMD on a Roth IRA, so it could grow tax-free for a longer period for your beneficiaries. That could be another reason for this to make sense when dealing with maximizing wealth transfer to the next generation.

9

PURPOSE PLANNING
GIVE/GIFT/SPEND

Our 2% Club clients aren't that worried about running out of money during their lifetimes; they're worried about running out of life.

What I believe this really means (after speaking with so many of them) is that they're worried about finding the purpose behind what they've worked so hard for. They don't want to regret all that hard work.

They've also started to realize they have financial freedom. They can do whatever they want, whenever they want, with whomever they want—because they have the money to do it. This is hard for the 2% Club to come to terms with because they've lived paycheck to paycheck most of their lives. They paid the bills and mortgage, provided for their family, and saved for retirement; there wasn't much discretionary income to live more abundantly. And that mindset of diligent focus on what was most important to them is what got them into the 2% Club in the first place. But now, in their retirement, with solid, predictable incomes, they're facing an extreme paradigm shift.

Most of the 2% Club are what I call "the best savers and the worst spenders." They're used to living extremely frugally. They worked their whole lives, carefully tucking away every extra dollar, skipping trips, saying no to dinners out, and always choosing the "responsible" option. Midwestern Millionaires hate spending money. Many of our clients may not want to spend money in retirement, and that's fine, but now, they have all this money saved up. What's the point of saving if there's no plan for the legacy it leaves behind? We talk about planning now to efficiently *give* and *gift* to their loved ones or to charities with missions they're passionate about. That said, some of our 2% Club members are thrilled with the "now we can spend" concept. They want to "have the last check bounce back" or "would rather fly first-class instead of having their kids fly first-class." This crowd needs to get busy spending! For them, we put together what we call a spending plan to go with their income plan. This ensures that they maximize their savings and spend the most they can in the way they choose—all without running out of money.

Give/Gift/Spend

So which group are you in? What would you do with your wealth at this point? The 2% Club has many options.

PURPOSE OF MONEY

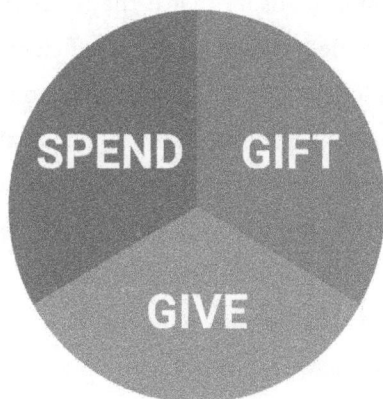

Give

Thinking about their favorite passions, missions, charities, or organizations is how our clients start the charitable *giving* part of this strategy.

For many of our clients, using their wealth to give could have a longer-term effect on a community or a cause important to them. If they gave $10,000 to a local charity, that may allow them to make a big difference. They can do this giving after they pass away or during their life. Many people consider giving while they're living so they can see the result of where it's going.

We also never encourage clients to only give because of the tax benefits—giving should come from the heart—but we do want to ensure that if they're going to give to charities, they do so in the most tax-efficient way, which could save a lot of money. There are even some strategies available that can result in more money in their pocket while also donating to a charity. Those are some of our favorite giving strategies.

The best advice we can give clients is to take action and put together a plan to ensure it happens the way they want. Too many times, we see people put off this conversation and planning. Then the money is left to the beneficiaries. Obviously, that's not the end of the world, but we always ask, "Is that really what you want?"

Gift

Our clients think of *gifting* in terms of giving money to their loved ones—their children, grandchildren, or others close to them—and not just when they pass away. Some clients are willing and able to get strategic and start gifting in their lifetime since they have excess savings from having a pension. There isn't only one way to do this gifting. How it's done is dependent on our clients' situation and mindset.

First, we explain the gift tax limits. In 2025 (the ceiling changes periodically), you could gift up to $19,000 per year per person without an estate tax consequence. Gifting to a child and their spouse doubles the gift. Maybe this is more than you want to give, but it is possible if someone wanted to be ultra generous.

It may be more effective to gift the money now when their children are raising a family of their own. Adult children might use the money to fund their retirement accounts, pay down any high-interest debt, build or increase an emergency fund, or pay taxes on a Roth conversion of a past 401(k).

Some of our clients in the 2% Club who choose to gift will skip a generation and go to the grandchildren. There are a few ways to do this, and not all are about gifting cash to the grandchildren. They can put money into an investment account for each of them; they can save for their education in an IRS-approved account, such as a 529 account, where they could now potentially move a portion to a Roth IRA in the future as well; or they can provide their grandchildren with travel and discovery experiences rather than with a cash or investment bequest.

We want to ensure that our clients are comfortable with the amount being gifted. There is no requirement to do this gifting. Some of our clients are concerned about gifting their children too much (we remind them that $19,000 is the *maximum* for tax purposes, not the *required* gift per year) and leading their children to not want to work or earn their own way. Many of our clients don't gift that much, but as you know, something could be better than nothing.

The choices always depend on our clients' specific situation and how they want to navigate it.

Spend

When we show our 2% Club clients how much they can *spend* per year in retirement, they tend to laugh and protest that they can't possibly spend all that. It's a testament to how well they've done but also to their disciplined mindset. It's the truth: Most of our clients can spend as much as they want in retirement.

Many do want to enjoy the fruits of their labor. Not all of them are worried about leaving an inheritance. They're the type of people who would rather see their loved ones work for everything they get ("like we did") versus giving it to them. We had a client tell us "I'm leaving this world the same way I came in . . . broke and naked." Those 2% Club members have some spending to do!

What could they spend this money on?

Most of the people we work with wish to do more traveling in their earliest retirement years, those Go-Go Years we mentioned previously. That could mean overseas trips or domestic trips to large US cities they've never discovered. It could mean roaming the country from one famous small town to another or seeing the heartland by car or RV via the legendary Route 66.

We had a client couple who spent $75,000 to go on a six-month cruise around the world—how about that? We've had others rent or purchase RVs to enjoy the great outdoors while traveling around the country at their leisure. Some have purchased a second home in another part of the country to spend half of the year there. One client bought a 1933 Auburn Speedster, their dream car. Others have rented a property that strikes their fancy so they can stay in that region for months at a time in more comfort than at hotels or in an RV.

At this point in their life, they may have more money than they have time, so they want to maximize that time. This could mean hiring a company or an individual to clean their house for them. They might stop doing their own landscaping or yard work and have someone else do it.

They might decide to spend more time and money on their health to ensure they can enjoy their later years. Maybe that means getting a massage every week or spending more money on healthier food. They might join a gym for the first time, where they can also book time with a personal trainer to get in better shape.

Some like to spend their money on their loved ones. Perhaps this means taking the family on a trip, allowing you to spend more quality time with them. Or getting a pool so you can provide a fun experience and joy for your family and friends.

All this is doable because of the diligent saving and hard work the 2% Club has done. The key is having a plan and taking action.

How Much Can Be Given, Gifted, or Spent Per Year?

Let's use something as simple as the 4 percent rule to give us an idea of how much a couple can take out of their investments on top of their pension and Social Security each year. The rule assumes that if they take out 4 percent from their investment accounts each year, they won't run out of money during their lifetime. There are many assumptions and factors associated with the 4 percent rule, but let's use it for now.

Let's say a couple has $2 million in investment accounts (savings), a $60,000/year pension, one Social Security benefit of $45,000/year, and another Social Security benefit of $25,000/year. This gives them $130,000/year of guaranteed retirement income from their pension and Social Security. Then, with the 4 percent rule, they could withdraw $80,000 ($2 million × 4 percent) each year from their investments to give, gift, or spend.

This would provide the couple with $210,000/year of income—probably more than they made in their working years, or at least fairly close to it. It's a generous place to be. Hopefully, this allows them the confidence to think about spending, gifting, and giving money during retirement.

Why work so hard for thirty to forty years or more and not see and experience the fruits of their labor? Too many diligent 2% Club members fail to find purpose with their money. Many times it's because they've never taken the time to plan for it or think about it.

We had a couple come to us at age sixty-two. They said, "We want you to help us put together a spending plan." When they had retired at age sixty, they swore to each other that they were going to get busy spending until age seventy-five. Why seventy-five? That was their expectation of good health and how long they could enjoy what they wanted to do. When they came to us, they said they hadn't done anything special in the last two years and regretted wasting time. They came to us to hold them accountable to live out their dreams in retirement. They discovered that their Midwestern Millionaire mentality was hard to break.

Sometimes it takes a team to give peace of mind and direction to ensure you live your retirement the way you want, with complete purpose—a purpose defined by you, your values, your goals, and your wishes.

CONCLUSION

The 2% Club has done the key things up to this point. They've awakened every day and gone to work, faced early mornings and late nights, been diligent about saving, and made sacrifices to get where they are today. They're exactly who we serve every day at Peak Retirement Planning, and we've gotten familiar with what they need and want.

Retirement is the time to maximize it all and enjoy the fruits of your labor, keeping as much money as you can and living the generous, comfortable life you've always imagined.

As I mentioned at the start of this book, my greatest hope is that you'll seek expert help with your retirement planning—or, at the very least, that you now understand what it takes to set yourself up for success. Whether you decide to work with us, a team like ours, or handle it on your own, the real secret is having a comprehensive plan—one that covers every pillar of pension planning we've discussed and takes into account the options you have with your pension.

Ignoring the 5 pillars could mean not optimizing your retirement, giving more money to Uncle Sam than necessary, and having less money to leave to heirs and beneficiaries.

The preceding image perfectly captures the idea of failing to plan. Sure, you could get through retirement by stacking your bricks in a chaotic, unplanned fashion. The wall would still go up and might even remain standing through the first couple of storms. But wouldn't you rather build an organized, foolproof wall that will withstand any storm over the long term? Having a retirement plan and working with a team will give you that and more—more clarity, more options, more tools, and ultimately, more peace of mind.

As mentioned, we work with a lot of people who "DIY" their retirement to this point. They often tell us they want to delegate their planning so they can stop worrying about it and enjoy their retirement. From what I've seen, I suspect DIYers could spend 100+ hours a year trying to do their own retirement planning. Staying on top of legislative changes and optimizing investments takes a lot of time. In addition, most DIY planners have never planned a retirement before, which means they must build out all the processes themselves and often worry they are missing things. Because they typically do not have access to the cutting-edge software and tools to make optimal decisions, they have to solve problems manually, which can take a longer time and still risk not being accurate.

One client came up to me six months after he made the decision to work with us and said, "I finally fully trust your team." He said he checked his investments and plan every day to ensure we were doing everything the same way (and better) than he would do on his own. After seeing our results, communication, and way of planning, he came to realize that he no longer had to worry about things, knowing we had everything in order. This gave him so much peace, as he had been wanting to offload this for years, but could not find a team he could trust. This benefited not only our client but also his wife, ensuring she had a trusted team if he were to pass away first. Trusting someone to help manage your life savings can be a tough decision, but when done successfully, as for many people, it becomes a worthwhile experience.

Many of those in the 2% Club want to know that they've built their retirement the right way and haven't missed any opportunities. What they're really focused on is first protecting and then maximizing their wealth: paying less in taxes, structuring their investments efficiently, ensuring their family is cared for when they're gone, and crafting a plan to fulfill their purpose and dreams.

A TEAM TO SERVE
YOU IN RETIREMENT

In these pages, I've been describing the 2% Club—the Midwestern Millionaire. The 2% Club's high income and high net worth place them in a rare category. Many of those in the 2% Club have come to us and said they couldn't find anyone locally who did this level of advanced planning for people like them.

We all want to work with "people like us," but also with people who bring expertise and experience to the table. Those we can trust and count on.

At Peak Retirement Planning, we prefer to specialize in pension planning for those with $1 million or more (only 2% of the population) than a jack-of-all-trades. We've decided to go all in with this niche category because it allows us to have extreme expertise and understanding of the 2% Club's needs, goals, and wishes.

That said, the 2% Club shouldn't only consult with an experienced team that offers a comprehensive, 5 Pillar, one-stop shop. They should also look for the 5 Pillars of pension planning all in one place: a firm where you have pension experts plus professionals who offer tax, investment, income, healthcare, and estate planning and where the experts in one pillar work with the experts in the other pillars on your behalf.

Working with a fiduciary team is extremely important. A fiduciary acts in the best interests of all clients, putting clients' interests ahead of their own. Thus, a fiduciary avoids conflicts of interest (like pushing specific investments or products when they don't serve the clients' best interest). In my opinion, the best standard to judge this is working with a team of CERTIFIED FINANCIAL PLANNERS™ (CFP®) .

At our firm, we require our advisors to either have their CFP® credential or be in the process of obtaining it. The CFP® is the gold star of the industry and holds advisors to the highest fiduciary standard possible. It also shows that they've done the work to understand everything in retirement planning. Not just in investments, but in the 5 pillars of pension planning discussed in this book.

Pension Planning with Peak Retirement Planning, Inc.

If you're in the 2% Club and looking for our kind of planning, feel free to go to our website to schedule a call to explore working with our team.

Currently, the average age of financial advisors is fifty-six.[17] This means that over one hundred thousand financial advisors are expected to retire within the next decade—roughly 40 percent.[18] At Peak Retirement Planning, however, we are an experienced younger team and will be here not only for our clients' retirement but also their spouse's retirement and their children's retirement (and we always joke that we'll probably be here for their grandchildren, also). This is one of the reasons I got into this career: I witnessed my mentor, a financial planner for forty years, serve four generations of families. Now that's having an impact.

As I always say, we're a family-feel business. My mom started the firm with me. I have a friend from fourth grade who works here. I have multiple friends from college on my team and many of our team members' family and friends

---

17   Morey Stettner, "Trust Your Money to a Young Financial Advisor? Increasingly You'll Have Little Choice," MarketWatch, updated June 22, 2025, accessed May 26, 2025, https://www.marketwatch.com/story/trust-your-money-to-a-young-financial-adviser-increasingly-youll-have-little-choice-1bf27425.

18   Usama Khan, "Average Age of Financial Advisors in America: Key Stats," Retirement Living, updated May 1, 2025, accessed May 22, 2025, https://www.retirementliving.com/financial-advisors/average-age-of-financial-advisors.

work with us as well. We want to extend that family feel to our clients.

We focus on building deep and strong relationships with the clients we serve and will not water down our service offerings. We promise our clients that when they entrust us with helping them manage their life savings, we are their partner. We respond within twenty-four hours when they reach out to us. We do quarterly touchpoints with them to ensure we are proactive and intentional in our 5 Pillar approach.

The level at which we serve clients takes a great amount of time and a team approach. We are continually hiring more advisors and team members to serve more families, but we only hire the best and not simply to grow. Our team is committed to being "the best, not the biggest." My mission was never to create an average financial planning firm to serve everyone. There are enough average financial planning firms out there that charge the same fees as we do, if not more, and offer their clients less. We want to be different and disrupt the industry, going above and beyond for our clients by providing exceptional service. I founded Peak Retirement Planning, Inc., to serve the 2% Club, those Midwestern Millionaires who hate taxes.

If that is you, schedule a time to explore working with us at Peak Retirement Planning, Inc. at:

www.PeakRetirementPlanning.com

And congratulations! Welcome to the prestigious 2% Club!

Oh, and don't forget: There is no U-Haul behind your hearse when you pass away, so get busy giving, gifting, or spending your wealth to achieve the most purpose from your hard-earned life savings!

"YOU CAN'T TAKE IT WITH YOU"

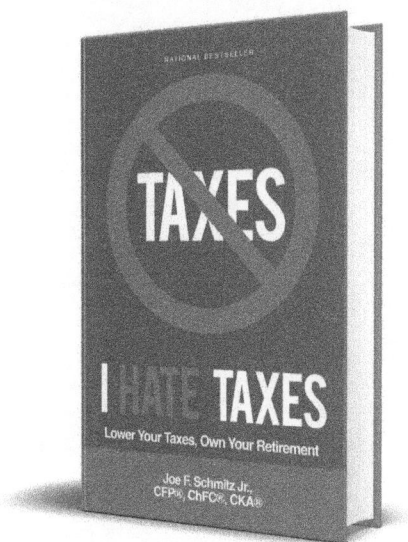

A Sneak Preview of Joe's National Bestselling Book,

I HATE TAXES

INTRODUCTION

Anyone may arrange his affairs so that his taxes shall be as low as possible; he is not bound to choose that pattern which best pays the treasury. There is not even a patriotic duty to increase one's taxes.

Over and over again the Courts have said that there is nothing sinister in so arranging affairs as to keep taxes as low as possible. Everyone does it, rich and poor alike; and all do right, for nobody owes any public duty to pay more than the law demands.

Learned Hand (1872–1961), judge, US Court of Appeals[1]

You know the old saying "It's not what you know but who you know"? Well, in my business of retirement planning, our saying is "It's not how much you *make*, it's how much you *keep*."

1   Gregory v. Helvering 69 F.2d 809, 810 (2d Cir. 1934), aff'd, 293 U.S. 465, 55 S.Ct. 266, 79 L.Ed. 596 (1935)

That's what this book is all about. You've worked hard all your life, but I can tell you without even knowing you or your situation that you're probably giving away much more of your hard-earned money to Uncle Sam than you need to.

People are vastly different, but there's one thing we all have in common, no matter our background, age, race, gender, belief system, or profession:

We all hate taxes.
And we all want to know how we can pay less.

Don't get me wrong. I'll pay my fair share of taxes. I love this country, appreciate my citizenship, and will pay my taxes accordingly. I'm grateful for the opportunities I have in this country and the ease of life my family and I enjoy.

So let's be clear: We're not talking about "tax evasion," which means breaking the rules. We're talking about "tax avoidance," which means being smart about what the rules say. This is about knowing what tools the US Tax Code makes available to us, using them properly, and paying only our fair share. We would never encourage you to do things that would send you to jail.

As a US citizen, your tax avoidance is not only legal but necessary. It's your patriotic duty. The less you send to the government, the more you can spend and invest the way you choose and the more you can control. That could create jobs and wealth for our economy. I see saving money on taxes as a way to invest in America and make it a better place.

If I can legally understand what the tax code says and find loopholes to save money, then what do you think I'm going to do? I work hard for my money, and so do you. This is your life savings we're talking about. We need to be as diligent as possible to keep more money in your pocket and less in Uncle Sam's. Because guess what? He's not your real uncle.

Now, if you enjoy paying taxes and want to pay more, I'm afraid this book isn't for you. You would be better off staying status quo and sending in a donation to the IRS every year above what you pay in taxes.

This book—and all the planning my firm does for our clients—is about how to limit Uncle Sam's take from your pocket in retirement.

My Two Goals for This Book

1. Motivate you to be proactive with your tax planning so that you have your own plan and not the IRS's plan.

2. Save you potentially $100,000+ in tax planning.

Don't tip Uncle Sam. Pay your fair share but not a penny more—keep your hard-earned life savings in your pocket.

CHAPTER 1

WHY ACT NOW?

Collecting more taxes than is absolutely necessary is legalized robbery.

Calvin Coolidge, thirtieth president of the United States, 1923–1929

To express the duty that you must pay the least amount of taxes—only the amount you owe—I went to the IRS website. The Taxpayer Bill of Rights literally includes, "The Right to Pay No More than the Correct Amount of Tax."[2]

The right! I will exercise that right to pay no more than the correct amount of tax.

The *I Hate Taxes* book title comes from one of our clients—I'll call her Jeannie—after she chose to trust us with her life savings. It was one of those memorable moments you never forget. Jeannie stopped me cold near the start of our

---

2   https://www.irs.gov/taxpayer-bill-of-rights.

session and looked me dead in the eye. Her voice raised, she said to me, "Joe, there's one thing I want you to know about me. I hate taxes. I don't like anything about them. I don't like how they're spent, and I don't want to pay for things I disagree with. I want to pay the least amount possible. I want to spend my money on what matches my values and beliefs, and I don't trust the government."

She's right.

The other problem with taxes is that sometimes they don't make sense. For example, tax benefits are given to people who make a positive impact on the environment, such as buying an electric car. Yet people are also given a tax benefit for buying a gas-guzzling RV motorhome, which has the opposite impact. A popular tax benefit is charitable gifting, which I heartily agree with and love what it can do for our country, but other benefits are less clear. Who's making these rules? Which rules are best? What are we truly incentivizing? Do the incentives match your values? Not always the case for me.

CHAPTER 2

WE'RE DIFFERENT FROM OTHER PLANNERS

I've made it my mission—and the mission of our firm at Peak Retirement Planning, Inc.—to help people pay the least amount of taxes over their lifetime. Our mission differentiates us from the masses, as many financial planners and CPAs won't talk about tax planning at all.

Tax planning isn't talked about enough.

Why aren't taxes talked about? For many, they'll be their biggest expense over their lifetime. Why then won't financial planners and CPAs bring these strategies to the table for you? We'll discuss why this is the case in chapter 20, so stay tuned.

Everyone's situation is unique. Married or single. Dependents or not. Deductibles or none. Different incomes make what I'm about to cite challengeable, but here goes:

Among the more than 164 million Americans who filed tax returns in 2020, the average federal income tax payment was $16,615, according to the most recent Internal Revenue Service data.[3]

Do the math over forty years of your active working life. That's $664,600. And that's an average of all tax-paying Americans. Ask yourself, did I even pay that much for my home? Not likely.

And still, many of you are scoffing, thinking that you've paid far more than that—and you would be right.

**Here's the real question to ask:
Did we need to pay that much?**

And here's the other question to ask: Are we truly paying our fair share?

If you review the following chart from the Tax Foundation website, it may show that you're paying well more than what others are paying. Fifty percent of taxpayers pay on average a 3.1 percent tax rate. I would imagine you're paying much more than that considering you're reading a book about hating taxes and saving money.

---

3   "How much income tax does the average American pay the IRS?" Liz Knueven, Business Insider, Updated February 1, 2023, https://www.businessinsider.com/personal-finance/average-federal-income-tax-payment-by-income.

High-Income Taxpayers Paid the Highest Average Income Tax Rates

Average Federal Income Tax Rate by Income Group, 2020

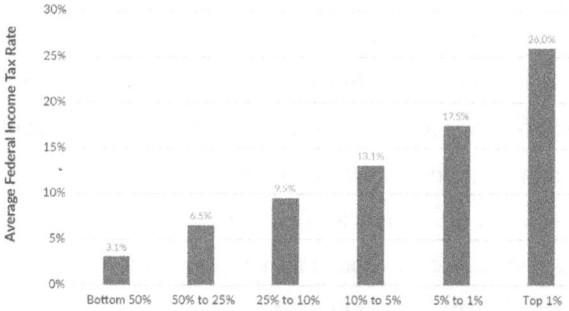

Source: IRS, Statistics of Income, Individual Income Rates and Tax Shares.

TAX FOUNDATION   @TaxFoundation

Source: "Summary of the Latest Federal Income Tax Data," Erica York, January 26, 2023, https://taxfoundation.org/publications/latest-federal-income-tax-data/.

I agree with the biblical reference of Luke 12:48, "To whom much is given, much will be required," and so I'll pay my fair share. But is it fair to penalize people who work hard and save money and reward people who don't work hard or save money? I would rather save money on taxes that aren't always used for my personal convictions and instead use that tax savings toward what I feel can make a true impact in this world.

> **If you hate taxes, don't avoid the IRS; instead, play their own game at an expert level.**

At Peak Retirement Planning, Inc., our experts know how to play (and win) the tax game. We know how to make an impact and help hardworking people keep their hard-earned life savings. Our firm delivers hundreds of workshops each year in our communities. We're constantly putting out content via our *Joe Knows Retirement* YouTube channel and podcast, TV, radio, articles featured in Kiplinger, and the books I write. I've seen too many people pay more taxes than they should, and we want to change that before it's too late.

During my years in financial planning, I've come to realize that there are two types of people who don't pay taxes: poor people and smart people. If you're poor, you reach a point where your income is so low that the government doesn't ask you for income taxes. If you're smart, you could live a tax-free retirement by understanding the rules and giving yourself enough time to plan. Being smart doesn't involve being poor.

We have a widowed client right now, Sarah, who has $1 million in her retirement accounts and will pay no more taxes for the rest of her life. This is what she and I call "legally divorcing the IRS for the rest of your life."

Sarah certainly isn't poor, but extremely smart financially. She has followed our advice over the years to get to where she needs to be. You may have heard that the rich also don't pay taxes. This annoys some, but I applaud them for being smart. The rich don't pay taxes because they hire smart people to show them strategies to reduce their taxes. Maybe you should do that yourself.

It's not what you know but who you know, right? Not only that: It isn't how much you make, it's how much you keep.

In short, when it comes to the rich, don't hate the player, hate the game.

There are loopholes in the US Tax Code for everyone— if you're smart enough to find them.

And, if like Sarah you have over $1 million net worth, then you're in the top 10 percent of our country's wealth.[4] Hate it or love it, you're wealthy. And most of your wealth is in tax-deferred investments with your partner Uncle Sam.

You better get busy planning. Hundreds of thousands of your dollars are on the line. If you're a saver and have done the right thing, then you're being desensitized. The tax system has penalized savers and benefited non-savers. That's criminal, if you ask me. The IRS can change the rules on us at any time.

Change Is Hard

Sometimes we know we need to change, and we don't want to. For some, you might know you need to eat healthily, but

---

4   "33 Incredible Millionaire Statistics [2023]: 8.8% of US Adults Are Millionaires," Abby McCain, February 24, 2023, https://www.zippia.com/advice/millionaire-statistics/.

you would rather go for the dessert, or you might know you need to get off your phone or social media, but you can't because you're addicted.

When it comes to taxes (and other things), inaction is the worst kind of action. The biggest advice I can give you through this book is to *get help*. The US Tax Code is complex. There are more words in the tax code than the Bible. Do you know what all the words mean? Have you ever even read it? If not, you're at risk of losing money and susceptible to government control, with less money in your pocket long term.

I cover tax-planning strategies in this book and will try to make them seem easy, but understand there is much more to it, and I'm only providing general information. Everyone's situation is specific, and everything I say in this book will be different for different people.

In my life, I try to delegate everything I'm not an expert at. I go to a doctor to perform surgery on me, I go to a mechanic to change my oil, and I have a team clean my house. I'm not good at cleaning, and I don't want to spend five hours on a Saturday doing it. I would rather spend my Saturdays writing tax books.

My point is, are you really going to have the time to understand how to make the smartest decisions financially with a full-time job, family responsibilities, hobbies, and other obligations? From what I see, that's a recipe for disaster.

If you're not on top of tax planning, you could miss saving hundreds of thousands of dollars over your lifetime. My goal with this book is to create a paradigm shift. Everyone is telling you not to pay taxes, but I'm going to tell you to pay your taxes now so you don't have to pay them later.

The IRS's Plan or Your Plan?

You have a decision to make. You can follow the status quo and ignore the opportunities at your fingertips—what we would consider the IRS's plan. The IRS's plan could cost you lots of money in mistakes over time as discussed earlier. Or you can follow your own plan where you know what's being done and when it's being done. Your plan could save you money on taxes. At the end of the day, your actions will decide your financial future.

ABOUT THE AUTHOR

Joe F. Schmitz Jr., CFP®, ChFC®, CKA®, is the founder
and CEO of Peak Retirement Planning, Inc., which was
named the number 1 fastest growing private company in
Columbus, Ohio by Inc 5000 in 2025.

Peak Retirement Planning, Inc. serves those in "The
2% Club" by providing their 5 Pillars of Pension Planning,
which includes tax-efficient strategies, investment
management, income planning, healthcare planning, and
estate planning.

As a CERTIFIED FINANCIAL PLANNER™, Joe has passed a rigorous education program and certification exam to receive the CFP® designation, and he has also spent over six thousand hours of professional experience to meet the CFP® experience requirements. Joe has also received the Certified Kingdom Advisor (CKA®) designation, demonstrating that he has learned the finer points of retirement planning, investing, insurance, and taxation in accord with Christian principles. He has created a firm that helps his clients have a deep sense of purpose in how they steward their wealth.

Joe got his start in the financial services industry in 2015. He graduated with a bachelor of science in finance and financial planning from Mount Vernon Nazarene University, where he also played basketball and ran track.

Known as a thought leader in the industry, he is featured in Kiplinger and various TV news segments. He is the author of the best-selling books *I Hate Taxes* and *Midwestern Millionaire*. You may have also seen Joe on YouTube, where he has one of the largest educational retirement planning channels for those in or near retirement with $1M+ saved and pensions.